Pr
with No Place to Hide

"This is a book that is sure to inspire others. It is full of hope and possibility. Pastor Van der Meer's journey is defined by her determination to overcome the troubles of the world and find meaning, purpose, and peace. *Out on a Limb with No Place to Hide* offers a fresh, insightful perspective on being a woman in ministry from the voice of one nurtured in the Caribbean culture of her native Trinidad and trained in the complex and sometimes political culture of American religious life. Through it all she has followed her own path. You will enjoy journeying with her on that path."

Pamela Ogletree
CEO of Children's Services of Roxbury
and Professor Charles Ogletree Harvard University

"*Out on a Limb with No Place to Hide* brings together the events of the author's life in a praise dance and song of cathartic memory in a restoration of spiritual health. Her catharsis is a personal dynamic, a purgation that endlessly reworks and transforms the pattern of personal experience and spiritual identity. The way this book sheds some light on the elusive meaning of atonement to transform personal experience increases awareness of how each of us can have access to its phenomenal journey to creativity and to spiritual enlightenment and growth. This is a courageous book and delivers on the underlying assumption that letting go is of vital concern to faith and one's sense of place and fulfillment. This book in its lyrical history of the author illuminates a current discussion of growing up female, but it is overwhelmingly about searching for one's place and finding sanctuary on the mountain top, which to borrow from the title is no place to hide."

Kenwyn Crichlow is an artist and a lecturer
Department of Creative and Festival Arts
University of the West Indies.

"I have known Reverend Van der Meer for several years as my co-worker in our hospital research review board. She shows herself to be a well-educated, disciplined, and professional person. After reading *Out on a Limb with No Place to Hide,* I can understand clearly how she has come to be a truly respected and loved individual. Her history proves to be one of the more remarkable stories that, as an American, growing up in American society, one can never fully grasp until Dianne put it in print. That's what stood out about her book—the real-life drama that brings out the reverend's charm, intelligence, and perseverance. I'm sure all who read her book will find it encouraging and uplifting."

Roger Gorman, M. D.
Chairman Institutional Review Board
West Boca Medical Center
Boca Raton, Florida

"Dianne's book will keep you right on the edge of your seat with her 'real life' incredible experiences. You will be hanging on to and riveted to every word—so that you won't want to put this book down until the very end! This book certainly is a must read for anyone who needs hope and is experiencing great challenges in their life and on the brink of despair!"

Bishop Frank E. Kelley
Way of the Cross Church
Boston, Massachusetts

Out on a Limb with No Place to Hide

Exposing Defeat While
Rising to Victory

Out on a Limb with No Place to Hide

Dianne
Van der Meer

Tate Publishing & Enterprises

This title is also available as a Tate Out Loud product. Visit www.tatepublishing.com for more information.

This book contains descriptions of situations and events that are recounted as accurately as possible from the author's memory. The names of those involved may have been changed in order to protect their privacy.

The opinions expressed by the author are not necessarily those of Tate Publishing, LLC.

Published by Tate Publishing & Enterprises, LLC
127 E. Trade Center Terrace | Mustang, Oklahoma 73064 USA
1.888.361.9473 | www.tatepublishing.com

Tate Publishing is committed to excellence in the publishing industry. The company reflects the philosophy established by the founders, based on Psalm 68:11,
"The Lord gave the word and great was the company of those who published it."

Cover design by Joey Garrett
Interior design by Stephanie Woloszyn

Published in the United States of America

ISBN: 978-1-60604-949-5
1. Inspirational Autobiography
2. Female Ministers, Caribbean Culture, Childhood Memoir
08.08.19

Dedication

This book is dedicated to my teenage daughter, Nzinga, who has stood her own ground on the battlefield with me and won the position of being, not only my beloved daughter, but friend, ally, and armor bearer. And, to my sons, Kashaka and Atiba, who, while they may not have always understood the pathways of my life's journey, stood with me, and at times, fended for themselves, determined to make me a proud mother.

While realizing that this memoir was written about me, in many ways it was also written for me. Its completion brings a sense of personal gratification, knowing that I will no longer be counted among the millions of procrastinators who had a story to tell but never quite got around to telling it. The cost of not having such regret is dedicated as my cherished reward.

In addition, I dedicate this book to the numerous men and women who in this end-time are called to establish churches all over Europe, the Caribbean, North America, Asia, and Africa. Let the peace of Christ rule in your heart and remember others have gone before you, trusting God. I did.

Acknowledgments

I want to take this opportunity to publicly thank my dear friend Karen Ruffin and the Ruffin family for their understanding in allowing Karen the time to edit my writings. Karen, you have helped me to keep alive my dream of completing this book. You have been of tremendous support and encouragement to me. Thank you, my sister.

Special thanks to my wonderful and charming mother, Yvonne Corentin. I would not have gotten this far without your prayers, counsel, and love.

Thank you, my dear brother, Glen Bernard, for believing in me and encouraging me to keep on.

To Pastor Novelett Robinson, Pastor Herman Bryant, Norma Duncan, Sister Ann Thorne and minister Dorothy Akuffu. Thanks for praying me through.

To my friends, Dr. Barbara Coulibaly, Pamela Ogeltree, Susan Shea, Dr. Linda Ostrander, and all my well-wishers, thank you for the encouragement.

Thank you, Uncle Lennox, Aunts Judy and Marjorie, and my dear friend and confidant, sister Gemma Maharaj.

Thank you, staff at Tate Publishing.

Thank you, Atiba, Kashaka, and Nzinga.

Atiba, your daily long-distance telephone calls with words of encouragement, love, and caring gave me strength.

Nzinga, just knowing that you were expecting me to give you a daily report, when you came in from school, of how many pages I had written that day motivated me to work. I will always remember the sight of you lifting your right hand, fist folded, and your shout of "Wow!" when the report was good. Daughter, some days the only factor that motivated me to work was in anticipation of your "Wow!" Hey, girl, thanks. Wow!

Kashaka, my son, you asked me the same question periodically, over the last thirteen years, "Mummy, when are you going to publish your book?"

Well, son, here it is. Enjoy!

Table of Contents

Foreword

In *Out on a Limb with No Place to Hide*, a memoir from the author Reverend Dianne Van der Meer, the author shares with the reader her journey of confirmation with her faith. The combination of experiences including molestation, gender exploitation and discrimination, racial bias, and single parenting all help to shape this woman, who at times seems to be embattled as she moves along a path of ever strengthening faith. While both dramatic and traumatic, are such experiences extremely rare? Surely, the combination must be unusual if not unique. At the same time, we might speculate that the occurrence of any one of these challenges happens much more frequently than one might suspect. Indeed, in many ways we should be appreciative that we have the privilege of reading this book to remind us of this fact. If we are correct about the suspicion that such factors and experiences are more prevalent in shaping the development of many individuals than to be assumed, then we can be encouraged by the author's experience. Her ability to conquer adversity while moving toward an ever strengthened faith and spiritual commitment is affirming.

The book is a serious exploration of one woman's efforts to reconcile her natural physical desires with her commitment to a lifestyle that exalts spirituality above all else. In some sense we see posed the age old dilemma of humanity's "weak flesh confronting seriousness of purpose and faith." What are the qualities of character that helps her move steadily along a positive path without giving in to despair and cynicism in the face of a series of disappointing behaviors, if not betrayals, by various males in her life? Perhaps it is her belief system, reverence toward a higher being and commitment to a higher calling.

This memoir certainly reveals much about the factors that influence Reverend Van der Meer's development. One suspects that her bi-cultural background has some impact on her ministry and how she approaches the many individuals that she helps, whether young or old. The reader is comforted by the obvious warmth generated in her lyrical description of her Trinidadian roots. One thing is apparent from the start of the narrative: although her influence is bound to extend beyond her island beginnings, she nevertheless will always reflect something about those experiences in her future relationships and activities.

Being called to the clergy, no doubt, involves a very personal journey for anyone. The relationship between the individual and his or her God is subject to someone else's analysis only to a very limited extent. We know that that relationship must be primarily spiritual rather than analytical. Reverend Van der Meer's story from childhood to the present is rich and varied. It is sweet and bittersweet, pleasurable and painful, intellectual and spiritual, yet always grounded in forgiveness and the love of family and friends.

She brings to the narrative first the perspective of an innocent little girl who is vulnerable and subject to exploitation but in possession of a certain inner strength even at a tender age. Later the vicissitudes inherent in the experience of a young woman being pursued by a sexually charged but immature man form an important element to her development cycle. To Dianne's credit, she evolves without harboring bitterness, hate, or anger. Her life as a mother, divorcee, and finally a single parent ultimately prepares her for her calling as a minister.

This book is very much a memoir in that it focuses entirely on the author's personal narrative. She does not seek to explore the personalities or character of the others whom she tells us have influenced her life. This decision to focus in a single-minded manner on her own story is both understandable and useful. The trauma that is inherent in the various experiences of Reverend Van der Meer constitutes an interesting story in itself. While it undoubtedly would have been interesting to know more about the motivations and character traits of those who impacted Dianne's life, these features are not integral to this very personal story.

Out on a Limb with No *Place to Hide* reaches into the soul of the author and out to the heart of the reader in an inspiring real life story of how one woman was able to conquer various life challenges, through faith, in spite of daunting obstacles. It is always refreshing to be able to rise up from defeat and disappointment as Dianne did, to embrace faith and hope as a good citizen.

James Hoyte
Associate Vice President
Harvard University
Cambridge, Massachusetts

Introduction

This book was written for the young at heart. I had a divine revelation to write it for the purpose of encouraging others. It captures the depths of my life in accounts that will make you laugh, cry, and even doubt and goes beyond my journey as a minority and woman in ministry. This memoir is different because it is not all about me. While each chapter is not directly linked, in terms of a story line or plot, each description shares a common thread—lessons learned, sorrow, laughter, risk, and faith.

In one chapter I share my teenage rape experience and how I refused to be confined to a box of guilt as I identified with women in the bible who suffered similar ordeals. Another chapter includes a guideline manual for praise dance as a form of worship and healing. I discuss my personal account as a participant and observer in street ministry. I recount my childhood dreams of leaving the small beautiful Caribbean island of Trinidad and Tobago to access higher education in America and recall my culture shock and experiences in adjusting to the host culture as a newcomer. In addition, I share the pleasurable and memorable experience of mountain climbing as a little girl in a little boys' world. I touch on my marriage, divorce, and single parenting and how I was able to finally position myself for God's use. I conclude with a must-read collection of advice from interviews that I conducted among church planters, rabbis and priests in Boca Raton, Florida, across the United States, and internationally.

Life on the Outside

My friend, Barbara, asked me, "What's the topic of your book?" *Topic,* I thought. "It's about me," I blurted, with fear in my voice at the thought of attention being turned toward me. "Well, I would like to read the finished product," she said. Then she paused. I could tell that she was waiting for me to continue. I broke the silence by asking her, "Are you fishing for a plot?" Her infectious laugh suggested yes. I pondered for a moment. "There is no central plot. This is my memoir," I said. "It reflects various aspects of my life journey. I don't like talking about myself," I continued, smiling. "It is always easier talking about someone else, wouldn't you say?" Perhaps the only logical central theme to this book is life on the outside. It is a place where many are afraid to go, a place where the rules are always changing and the risks are high.

I have been on the outside from birth. My mother was often sick during her pregnancy with me. Without the benefit of ultrasound, she was not aware that I was a breech birth until she struggled to save my life and hers with the help of the village's experienced midwife. I had the benefit of an anointed praying grandmother who prayed me to the outside, prayed the lingering placenta out of my mother, and nursed us both back to health.

Life on the outside all started for me in that dimly lit back room of my grandmother's house on the Caribbean island of Trinidad. I later asked my mother why she decided on a home-birth since, if I had had my say, I would have much preferred the security of medical science at the hospital. She told me that it was a privilege to be born at home and that she was confident in my grandmother's ability to pray down heaven should the need arise. My mother told me that the midwife silently stared into her placenta like a scientist observing through a microscope. Finally, the silence was broken, and the midwife said, "You will never be able to have another child." The midwife never said why and my mom, at age twenty-three, was too scared and weak to ask. My mother fought for the next twenty years to have another child, but she never did. It seems as if I had beaten the odds from birth.

My Earliest Memory

My earliest memory is of when I was five. I recall Ma (my grandmother) cooking food and feeding the poor. My grandfather (Pa) was a self-made successful businessman who converted from Hinduism to Christianity to be able to marry his teenage sweetheart.

Pa practiced real estate, exported fruits, and imported turkey and dried foods. A jack-of-all-trades, he was also a moneylender and earlier in his career, owned and rented fishing boats. His gateway into business was as a commercial fisherman. Long lines of homeless people would flock outside of our home every Friday to receive money and sometimes a home-cooked meal. I remember Pa always giving me the money to give to the poor. A few pennies were given to each person, but a penny in 1961 went much further than a penny spent today. This practice continued for a few years until I was about nine, when both grandparents got sick and Pa died.

It was always an excitement and pleasure for me to help others. I felt special as those poor and homeless men and women gave blessings to their God in different dialects and hand language. Some made the sign of the cross, while others openly praised the Hindu goddess Lakshmi. I sometimes became overwhelmed and other times fascinated. I could vividly remember my heart being full of compassion entangled with the joy of giving. It's a combination that confused my five-year-old mind. I did not know whether to be happy or sad. The image of outstretched hands and sometimes a faint smile beaming through war-torn wrinkled faces in the hot noonday Caribbean sun was imprinted in my imagination.

It was only in my adult years that my aunt Marjorie told me the story of how Ma and Pa got involved in homeless care. She said that when I was four, my family discovered that I gave to a homeless woman in the neighborhood my weekly pocket change that my uncles gave me. I gave away pennies that my grandfather saved in a brown paper bag, which he kept in his bedroom. Although I knew nothing of the movie character Robin Hood, I sure had some of his qualities, by stealing from the more fortunate and giving to the less fortunate. This is not an endorsement for Robin Hood. I was just a babe!

Auntie Marjorie captivated my attention when she shared with me that I graduated to hiding food to give to this homeless woman as she passed by our house. The woman, in return, would share her rotting fruits with me. Realizing that this was an unhealthy situation, my family attempted to stop me, only to catch me in the act of giving to this woman again. By this time, the homeless woman had begun to bring a couple of her friends, and I kept on sneaking to give. One Friday, my money ran out, and Pa came home just as the women were approaching the gate, so I could not run inside and raid his brown paper bag. I shouted to Pa to come and give these homeless women money but instead he ran inside. He argued with Ma, accusing her of encouraging me to give away all of our money. My aunt said that I did not give up but stood by the gate shouting for Pa to bring me more money to give to the homeless. When he would not budge, I started to hysterically cry and demand that Pa "bring the money." Apparently, some of that drama queen theatrical trait still lingers in my life when I can't have my own way. Finally, Pa "broke." He gave in and sent Ma to bring me inside. Aunt Marjorie gave out the money to the eagerly waiting homeless women. This started the practice of my family feeding and financially helping the marginalized in our society. Aunt Marjorie's details connected for me the long lines of homeless people that gathered at our gate when I was a child.

Mountain Climbing

In my early teens, I enjoyed the sport of mountain climbing. Without the appropriate safety gear, my neglect of safety was purely out of ignorance. We never knew about using climbing gear and proper shoes. These few adventure trips remain the best experiences of my life. In a male-oriented society I was breaking new ground as a female and at the same time reaching my goal of standing at the top of the mountain. Our culture viewed mountain climbing as a male sport and totally unorthodox for females. Girls were supposed to prepare to become caretakers, nurses, teachers, and of course, stay-at-home moms.

I always looked forward to summer because school vacation meant going to visit my auntie Marjorie and being able to mountain climb. She lived in the mountainous tropical rain forest of Dibe on the island of Trinidad in the West Indies. Her house was perched high on Cumberland Hill just beyond the base of the Northern Range. Vacationing in Dibe gave me a sense of belonging. My aunt had six children, and we all played together. My favorite cousin of the six was Irmin, because she always seemed like she was reaching for the unreachable. It was a feeling of community.

In Dibe we didn't have the comforts of home. It was like a permanent summer camp in the wilderness with lots of love, comradeship, adventure, and bonding. My grandmother's sister and her extended family also lived in Dibe, and some evenings we would gather at their house for storytelling. It was special. My cousin Earl would always make up stories to scare me. It worked. One of Earl's stories was about the creature that appeared in the outhouse after dark. You can figure out who never had to use the outhouse after dusk. It made me so scared that during my "camp" stay, my bowels only functioned in daylight!

Food seemed to be always in rationed portions at my aunt's house, but the love was in abundance. Many times we divided up a few mangoes or other seasonal fruits for breakfast. Fried bakes (dough made from flour, salt, and water and deep-fried) were served for lunch as a welcome alternative.

It often rained in Dibe. I reminisce about the view of mist gently and weightlessly floating among the flora and fauna, creating the rain forest effect that gave a feeling of ecstasy. On a dry day, one great way to pass the time was to catch tadpoles in the stream and chase butterflies. Butterflies of every color and species could be observed effortlessly floating in the breeze. Sometimes I got sad and homesick and would sit alone at the river. There, in the surrounding bushes, lizards of every size, from tiny green geckos to massive iguanas whisked in and out of the trees and shrubs. It felt like a glimpse of heaven.

Plants of every variety lined the landscape of Dibe. Many were used by the locals for medicinal purposes. For the common cold we were given the homemade remedy of hot tea made from Buckcano leaves. The leaves were boiled with dried prunes and the peel of an orange and then sweetened with honey. I remember that potent potion being quite tasty. And it worked. I enjoyed learning about the names of herbs that were used for medicine. My experience in Dibe was a rich informal education that helped shaped my life and is worthy of my recollection. It was the mountains of the Northern Range that surrounded Dibe that fascinated me the most.

The mountains gracefully stood along the periphery of Dibe in royal silence. Upon reflection, they remind me of my feeling of wanting to pinch the guards at Buckingham Palace in England, to see if they were really human or borrowed from the wax museum. Like these guards, the mountains seemed untouchable and unreachable. The aura of the mountain enticed me and awoke my curiosity. It called to me as if to say, come, climb. I called back to it by inwardly telling myself I would. I persuaded my cousin, Wayne, into taking me along with his friends to climb Cumberland Hill of the Northern Range. It's a trip that Wayne and his two friends often made to harvest mangoes. Wayne would always say that the tastiest mangoes were the ones that grew deep in the forest and high on the mountain. I quickly agreed with his theory to gain his favor. The three boys' goal was to get various types of mangoes, especially the prized calabash mango. Oh yes, I wanted to taste a good calabash mango, but my goal was to conquer the mountain.

I had a dream the night before my victory virgin climb. In the dream I saw myself getting out of breath climbing in the hot noonday sun with sweat running down my forehead. A brush fire was ahead of me, and I desperately looked around for my cousin. Suddenly, there was also fire behind me, and my visibility was impaired. I found myself alone with the elements of nature and my desire to live. *Do I go forward or backward?* The thought flashed through my mind. I was not about to be defeated, so I charged forward, leaving what was behind me in the distance. I could now feel the scorching heat like magma sprung from Volcano Souffiere on the Caribbean Island of Saint Vincent. A determination came upon me to conquer this mountain, and I was not about to give up. But would I die pursuing a dream, disintegrate in the heat, and never to be heard from again? Maybe I would, but it would be because of the personal satisfaction of not giving up. As I pressed forward, I could hear the sound of helicopters and saw the planes spraying sheets of white water to control the fire. Trapped in the wind, the water erratically danced, struggling to hit its target. It looked like a losing battle. I was still aggressively approaching the fire, searching for a way out, like hurricane chasers seeking the eye of a vicious hurricane. I could hear the twigs popping and see tree limbs falling like flies sprayed with a potent chemical. The wind blew and suddenly engulfed me with a violent sweep. I helplessly closed my eyes in anticipation of death. When I felt released from the jaws of the wind, I slowly opened my eyes. The fire was still blazing, but now I was sitting on the top of the mountain in a calm silence looking down at the raging fire. Mission accomplished, I felt like an Olympic gold medalist waiting to hear her nation's anthem play. Then I woke up. I lay on my bed awaiting daybreak, more eager to conquer the mountain.

At daybreak I reached for my toothbrush, but I could not find it. I got out of bed and proceeded to the nearest tree to pick a twig as a substitute. I fetched a cold cup of water from the barrel to rinse my mouth. It shocked my gums, tongue, and teeth. The dew drops were still fresh on the leaves. The sound of birds in the stillness gave the feeling the world had stopped on its axis. The fog had settled over the mountain like angel hair over a Christmas tree. The air was fresh, and I took deep breaths. I felt invigorated.

It was time for the climb. My two female teenage cousins, who were around my age, had to settle for playing dollhouse, while *I* was going to touch that which seemed untouchable. Our team of four gathered in my aunt's front yard. I gazed at the mountain in awe. Wayne, the self-appointed leader, gave orders and did last-minute checks. He checked the size of the bag I would use to collect mangoes and said that I must stay close to him and follow his orders. I quickly agreed because I was not about to be left behind. Off we went.

The climb started from the hill at the back of my aunt's house. We used no safety gear, no ropes or special shoes with grips, no electronic devices, cell phones, or radio monitors. No one checked the weather forecast for that day. There was no sophistication in our approach to climbing this mountain, just the wisdom of teenage boys who learned the climb from doing it. Life was so simple yet so meaningful. I was happy. We used a trail that led past Aunt Marjorie's outhouse and followed it for the climb. I stopped by a spring to admire the Balisier plant and its beautiful flower. The locals believed that the Balisier and cocoa plants attract snakes. Realizing that we were surrounded by both plants, I got scared. But in defense of my gender, I stayed my course. I reached cautiously and picked cocoa pods. One boy opened a pod, and we sucked on its sweet pulp, tossing the cocoa seeds away in total disregard of their value. Cocoa—in its rawest form, at my fingertips. We collected a few pods in our bags and continued the climb. It started to rain. I knew then that we were in trouble because we could hardly see an arm's length in front of us, and occasionally, one of us would slip and fall on wet leaves. I wanted to turn back but dared not suggest it.

There was a nervous silence as the group marched forward, and the three male egos seemed determined to prove their bravery. Mine was not far behind. Never once did anyone suggest turning back. The mountain was very slippery, and at times the place would get dark and misty. I never found out our altitude, but here I was on the mountain having mixed feelings. We were now at a narrow stretch. The only way across was to walk sideways and hold hands. There was a very deep drop that looked like the door to hell. One slip and we would have taken the plunge of death. Holding hands as a rope and taking small steps was the only way that we could navigate very narrow areas. I saw my mother and my bald-headed doll named Teardrops flash before my eyes. I wanted to cry but dared not. Danger lurked all around us as lightning flashed and thunder roared. I glanced at my cousin, who led the group. He looked scared as well, but no one was talking. One of the boys lovingly smiled at me and commented that I was doing well for a girl. I smiled back as if to say, I am not afraid because I am a girl. All I really wanted at that point in time was to be assured that I would see Teardrops again.

Drenched and cold we made it across that dangerous stretch. One boy proudly announced, "Choose," as we arrived at the site of mango trees. I looked up ahead and saw calabash mango trees laden with fruit, the joy of harvest. There were other types of mangoes and fruit trees in the area. I sank my teeth into an overripe mango, piercing the skin and letting the juice trickle down my hand. A bug landed on me as if to share my mango. I fanned it away with the other hand and thought, *Wayne sure knows how to choose mangoes.* I had never tasted a sweeter mango. It seemed to have gotten dark earlier than usual, so we started to quickly fill our bags and head home. The boys seemed impressed that I appeared unmoved by the inclement weather and rough terrain. Had I proven myself as a girl? Yes, and little did I know that this was only the beginning of the life challenges that I would face and win because I am female and refuse to have gender limitations set for me.

Mission accomplished, I conquered the silent royal mountain. We made it back safely but wet, muddy, and tired with mangoes and cocoa pods in hand and an experience of a lifetime. The trip bonded us as friends.

Cousin Wayne and I still share a special bond. What happened to the other two boys on the team? One succumbed to heavy drugs and the other, I am told, had a motorcycle accident that permanently affected his mental capacity.

The evening we returned from the climb, I showered using rain water that was collected in a big oil drum behind my aunt's house. I felt satisfied and settled in for a quiet evening with the girls. We played with our dolls, and I shared my mountain-climbing experience. Later that evening I took my doll Teardrops on a horseback ride through the imaginary ranch that I owned. I remember thinking that one day I could move away from my homeland and be whatever I wanted to be. I felt confident in myself, and my self-esteem shot up. At the tender age of ten, I felt accomplished and free to launch out and discover the future. The mountain climb removed the fear of defeat and increased my determination to succeed. I felt my life going to another realm as my imagination raced ahead of my tiny body. I knew then that this, for me, was life on the outside. There was no turning back.

Silent Cry

Where Is My Dad?

In my life I have had some silent cries, when I wanted to express my innermost feelings, but had to suppress it because I did not feel a freedom to share with those around me.

I cried silently for my father. I did not grow up with him because he and my mother separated when I was just a baby, but my dad remained a tangible presence in my life. My uncle Sparkey always told me that my dad loved me and that I was intelligent just like him. It was these thoughts that I internalized. They helped me to bond and connect with my father even in his absence. As a young girl, I thrived on seeking knowledge and excelling to maintain an identity like my father's. These thoughts were the motivating factor that kept me going. Albert Einstein said, "Imagination is more important than knowledge." My entire extended family would always tell me that one day I would be very successful because my dad is a brilliant man and I imagined myself being successful. My father spoke about seven different languages and was very active in state government. Sometimes, as a child, I could not always verbalize my true feelings about my dad, but I often wondered, *If he is so smart then why doesn't he act smart and come home?* But by this time, he had started another family and often visited me with my new brothers. He acted like an absentee property owner who periodically visited to ensure that his investment was secured. On reflection, I wondered whether his visits were for a dual purpose, including keeping tabs on my mother's personal life. He remained fond of her all his life and would often tell me how much he loved my mom. He was one of those men who wanted to have his cake and eat it, too. My mom told me, and as I grew, I observed for myself that my dad had a serious drinking problem and was a heavy social drinker before they met. She eventually moved on with her life and married my stepfather, whom I also loved and respected. Both men died within three months of each other, and I had the privilege of doing the eulogies at both their funerals. I described my biological dad as a small man with a big heart who wanted the best for me. I said of my stepfather that he was the best dad ever. I was blessed to have shared two dads and two moms in a very positive experience.

I silently cried for my dad as I watched my cousins playing with their father. I realized that I was missing that interaction, and I wanted it. I remembered my aunt's husband, Lincoln, would always bring back home a little leftover lunch in his three silver enamel lunch containers stacked one on top of each other. That's the only time my cousin Marlene would refuse to play with me. When she saw her dad coming with his lunch containers swinging in the wind, she knew it was time to eat and more so, get attention from her dad. She and her younger sister, Stephanie, would fight each other for the opportunity to hug Dad and hold the container. I imagined how the feeling would be like for me had it been my dad. It was at these times when I silently cried. I dealt with it by pretending I did not need a father and it did not matter if he was dead or alive.

When my dad actually died, I was about forty-five years old, and in the days leading up to his burial I missed him but could no longer pretend. At the funeral I insisted on being a pallbearer with my five brothers. I would have snatched him out of the coffin and brought him back to life had it been possible. At the gravesite I uncontrollably wept as I reflected on how he missed my life and I his.

I reflected on my failed relationships with men and finally admitted to myself that it was not just about my wrong choices or incompatibility. My lingering desire to have a father in my life made me slightly overpossessive and insecure in every relationship. Once, my husband said to me, "Dianne, you are driving me insane with your jealousy." He reassured me by saying, "Just look at how beautiful you are," holding my face directly in front of the mirror. I was secretly afraid to lose the man in my life, and when I did, I mustered up the strength to keep on going, pretending that it did not matter. Now, standing at the head of my dad's coffin, it all mattered.

Every tear penetrated my smokescreen, and in a miraculous way I felt a healing from the fear of rejections.

I felt the love of my father as if his spirit were hovering around the cemetery saying to me, "Daughter, I loved you all along." I could feel the love in my heart for him and appreciated my own beauty because my dad loved me and Jesus loves me. Someone shouted to my brother, Glen, "Move her from there," apparently fearing that I would fall or throw myself into the six-foot hole with the coffin. Glen shouted back, "No, just leave her alone." Thanks, Brother Glen, for allowing me my final moments and conversation with my dad. Amazingly, I left the cemetery a different person. My self-confidence and self-esteem were restored, and I felt freed of some insecurity, promising never to be the jealous wife, should I remarry.

Teenage Rape

My next experience is a silent cry that haunted me for years, one from which I grew, learned lessons, and found strength to keep going. I was the victim of rape as a teenager, and the perpetrator was a close friend, neighbor, and schoolmate. Because of the rape, I suffered rejection on two levels; the first from the man who raped me and the second from the silence that I felt I was expected to keep because of cultural norms. My hope is that my expression of my innermost reflections on this period of my life will bring healing to others who have silently suffered the same plight. I hope they will speak out and seek healing.

I grew quite friendly with this young man from my neighborhood who was about six years my senior. For the purpose of this story, I'll call him Fred. We attended the same school for a short period. He was one of the most popular boys and a hot item for girls of every grade. Fred showed much interest in me, though I had made no effort to be his friend or to get his attention like all the other girls. I must admit though, his attention felt good, and it was a refreshing compliment to my sometimes low self-esteem. I felt a little notch up because of his attention. Fred lived in my neighborhood, and his mother was a friend of my mother's from childhood. When he graduated, he came back to school every day just to hang out. He apparently wanted to stay connected with his friends at school since he interacted with a lot of girls in the lower grades. Whatever his reasons for frequently returning to visit the schools, I would never know, but I was about to be drawn into his net without warning.

I became Fred's next target as he assured me that I need not worry about any of the other girls because he loved me and they were all jealous of me. I bought that lie because it was what I wanted to hear. Fred became my first boyfriend. He made me swear never to listen to any false rumors about him because all the girls lied about him, a case of "can't get the grapes, so call them sour." I felt special and disregarded even my best friend's warnings about this guy, believing her to be jealous also. I stopped giving her a daily report on my interaction with Fred.

Fred and I talked about life in the future and being together until "death do us part." We talked about our kids, swearing always to be there for each other. But my friends at school were singing a different tune about Fred. They said that all Fred wanted from me was to get into my panties. I could not believe this because he was always very polite, never forced me, and he respected my view on not having sex until we were married. Fred even commended me for my values. I grew to trust and love Fred and kept no secrets from him. When he asked me to tell him when my parents planned to go out on weekends, I was delighted to share their every move with him. Since we did not have any phones, this prior information worked well because he would sneak by the fence when my parents were out and we would chat, just chat. A few times he asked to come inside; but I knew that my parents would have a fit, and I might not have lived to tell this story. I kept telling Fred I could not let him in because I was afraid my sister would talk and get me in trouble. He seemed to understand.

One day, when my parents were out, Fred appeared unannounced, and I sneaked him into the house. He talked about how well kept the house was and asked for a guided tour. While in my parents' bedroom, Fred suddenly put his hands over my mouth and with all his strength tossed me on the bed. With his other hand he started to tear off my pants and blouse. I could not breathe, and my sounds were muffled. I fought like a tiger, but he overpowered me. He began to talk to me, telling me how much he loved me and that I must cooperate with him or he would hurt me. I begged and pleaded with him, but he proceeded to viciously rape and beat me. He was transformed into something that I did not know. Fred's faced looked like a demon that came straight from the pit of hell. He kept saying, "I know that you want this." I could only cry and say, "No, no, please stop." At one point in the ordeal, I felt so weak that I felt my spirit leaving my body. Fred, seemingly satisfied, left me bleeding and crying. He commanded me to get up and see him out the front door and to lock the back door. I was so scared that the sound of his voice had me obeying his instruction, walking behind him like a zombie.

When Fred left my house, I had to race to clean myself and my mother's bedroom before either my parents or sister arrived home. Then I had to pretend that all was well, but with each passing day I silently cried for years. I felt that it was my fault, but it was not. I felt dirty and ashamed. Fred had befriended me and robbed me of my precious virginity. I did not know how I would face friends at school that Monday morning because I felt as if everybody would know by just looking at me. I contemplated suicide.

The next day Fred came by the fence to tell me that he loved me and that I should never talk about the night before because it was all my fault. At that time, I believed it was my fault. I felt dirty and unworthy. Fred said if I didn't tell anyone, he would always be there for me. Once again, he appealed to my comfort level, and I felt that he was the only one who carried my secret and understood how I felt. I could not share my ordeal with anyone else because, culturally, in Caribbean families, the two least talked about subjects are rape and menopause. To a large extent, the same holds true in many cultures and societies in both third- and first-world countries. This lack of open discussion has traditionally formed a hotbed of muzzled truth and is the source of silent cries. For example, as a young adult I remembered when someone broke into my middle-aged neighbor's house and raped her. My own experienced flashed before my eyes early that morning when I heard the news. The news soon became community gossip, and I felt helpless, not having the resources and freedom to reach out to my neighbor. None of the adults in my community, to my knowledge, attempted to offer their support to this hurting woman. She relocated to hide her embarrassment and fear, and the subject died an unsolved death. The woman became semi-reclusive. In my case, over time I stopped eating, contemplated suicide, and developed a stomach ulcer. I became so dehydrated and suffered from chronic constipation, which requires a surgical procedure to remove stools. It was a long road back for me, but I had a will to live and succeed in life, so I just kept on going.

Today in the Caribbean the approach to dealing with rape is gradually changing through active education, a heightened sensitivity in the judicial system in the handling of rape cases, and by the pioneering work of activists for more friendly legislation for rape victims. Unfortunately, many churches' willingness to address the issue of rape and domestic violence is still light years away.

My involvement with Fred continued in a very dysfunctional love-hate and sometime sexual encounters. Over a year had passed since the initial incident. I got pregnant and shared the news with Fred. He battered me and then dumped me for another girl who seemed as innocent as I was when Fred and I had first met. I lost the baby. I bled heavily and cried inwardly. The rejection was worse than the rape and my loss. I turned to the Bible for relief. I said, "Jesus, if you are real, do not let me die, but help me to understand who you are and give me the strength to come out of this mess." By this time my grades at school were slipping, but I was still able to graduate.

I identified with the biblical characters Dinah and Tamar, two young virgins who, like me, were raped. Dinah was the daughter of Jacob and Leah. Shechem, the son of Hamor the Hivite, prince of the country, raped her. "And Dinah the daughter of Leah which she bear unto Jacob, went out to see the daughters of the land. And when Shechem the son of Hamor the Hivite, prince of the country, saw her, he took her, and lay with her, and defiled her" (Genesis 34:1–2, KJV). Dinah, after being raped, later became the wife of the rapist, who was not of the people of God. The Hivites were God's enemies. She settled for less because of her circumstances. I never wanted to settle for less because of mine. I certainly did not fault Dinah's brothers, Simeon and Levi, who took matters into their own hands and killed Shechem and Hamor, his father (Genesis 34: 25- 26). I knew that I had to move beyond my anger and blame if I was to get more out of life.

It was Tamar's story that most closely related to mine. The book of Leviticus 18:9–10 discusses Amnon, the son of David. Amnon's knowledge and disrespect of the Levitical law brought him into conspiracy. The law stated a man shall not uncover (have sexual relations) with his sister. The book of 2 Samuel 13:5 discusses Amnon, who conspired with Jonadab (his friend and cousin) to defile Absalom's sister, who was also Amnon's sister—a virgin named Tamar. The plan unfolded when the two friends concocted a lie. Amnon would pretend to be sick to trick his father, King David, into sending Tamar to cook for him. The unsuspecting king ordered Tamar, his virgin daughter, to visit the house of her supposedly sick brother, Amnon. While there, she prepared food. Amnon pretended to have lost his appetite and be too sick to eat his bread. But his real intention was to lure Tamar into his bedroom. He asked everyone, including his servants, to leave the room as he cleverly tricked his prey into his chamber. In verse eleven of 2 Samuel 13, Amnon startled Tamar by grabbing her and asking her to have sex. She felt endangered, as his words were demanding and his gestures were intimidating. In her wisdom, she tried to reason with him, but to no avail. Amnon refused to listen, overpowered her, raped, and then rejected her.

In the aftermath of Tamar's ordeal, she reflected on what was worse, the rape or the rejection. She concluded that it was the rejection. I have concluded that they are equally painful. In 2 Samuel 13:15 Amnon commands Tamar to get out of his face, in the same way that Fred once rejected me. Amnon wanted her to be gone. Tamar told Amnon, "… there is no cause: this evil in sending me away is greater than the other that thou didst unto me" (2

Samuel 13:16, KJV). But Amnon did not listen to her and summoned his servant to put her out of his house. Tamar suffered much loss. She could no longer claim prestige as the virgin daughter of King David. This meant she could no longer wear the clothes that signified she was a virgin and could no longer be offered in marriage to a prince or to nobility as was custom. She responded to this by retreating. Tamar resided in the house of another brother, Absalom, for the rest of her life. Absalom felt her pain, but their society was not ready to openly address rape. Absalom forbid Tamar from speaking about the matter. Absalom said to her, "'Has that Amnon your brother been with you? Be quiet now, my sister; he is your brother. Don't take this thing to heart.' And Tamar lived in her brother Absalom's house, a desolate woman" (2 Samuel 13:20, NIV). A couple of years later, Absalom took revenge by killing Amnon, but the damage to Tamar was irreversible. Tamar must have suffered a silent cry.

Upon reading these biblical accounts, I convinced myself that I was not going to fold up and vegetate like Tamar but was going to, with the help of the Lord, free myself from guilt, shame, and blame and get on with my life. Unfortunately, too many men and women have gone through life after rape like Tamar: bound to secrecy and brokenness, which shapes them into forever being victims. As a teenage rape victim, I had already begun to display character traits of fear and low self-esteem. I was determined to overcome these traits but continued to struggle with them into my adult years. I knew that my life was not to end like Tamar, Dinah, nor my middle-aged neighbor. I had to be free in my spirit. As an adult, my healing came when I went into a twenty-one-day self-designed fast and time of soul-searching. I started with a strict fast. I had no water or food for three days, getting up to pray at five in the morning daily, and praying a few times a day. Some days I stayed at home and spent the day praying and reading the bible. I actually cultivated a prayer pattern that lasted well beyond my twenty-one-day fast. On the fourth day, I consumed water and fruit juice and about the tenth day added small amounts of fruits and vegetables. It was during this fasting period that I formulated the life-search exercise.

1. I grouped my age in ten-year periods. For example, at forty years old, I had experienced four period cycles—birth to age ten, age ten to age twenty, and so on.

2. I reflected on each ten-year period, recording every major memorable occurrence. I wrote about my birth, missing my father, my marriage and divorce, and many happy times.

3. I individually recorded each experience from each grouping and tried to recall how I felt at that point in time. For example, was this a sad, happy, or frightening experience for me?

4. I looked at opportunity cost in my life—those things that I chose to give up for the benefit of something else. For example, it was more profitable for me to give up enjoying social evening at work

with a few girlfriends in favor of attending weekly Bible study and youth night at my church.

5. I then laid out all my findings in groups for comparison and looked for any reoccurrences and similarities across groups, to identify the connecting threads.

6. I identified my weaknesses and traced them to their source using my life experiences. It was a journey through life, fishing for broken or weak links in order to repair them and to identify my strengths. This step particularly helped me not to make the same mistakes in life.

As I tabulated my data and analyzed it, I discovered that fear and insecurity were the two constant factors in this life-search exercise. I realized that I was not healed from the fear of teenage rape and was still blaming myself. I began to see how these experiences shaped my thinking and influenced my personal choices.

The key to the life-search exercise is that I now had specifics to take to the Lord in prayer. I had a glimpse of the inner me and was ready to address myself in an open, prayerful non-denial mode. Once I recognized my own shortcomings, I could begin to address them in a healing process. It is this clearing away of baggage that prepares us for the master's use. My life-search exercise made me much more sensitive to the working of the Holy Spirit. After decades of hurting from the rape experience, I broke my silence and talked to God about this and other matters that affected my life. My goal was to achieve a sense of physical and spiritual oneness in the process of healing.

I went to the master healer with my sacrifice of fasting. I made a commitment to meet God before sunrise every morning to show him that I was serious about giving him my firstfruits and tapping into my healing. I needed the Holy Spirit to unlock the prison of my heart and mind. At times, I knelt before the Lord and could not speak. I just wept and groaned. My language of tears wet my living room sofa. I asked, "Why me, Lord?" After I was finished with my pity party, I felt that my deep-seated hurts and problems were exposed, finally coming to light like exposing a skeleton in the closet. As my early mornings with Jesus went by, I began to totally surrender. It was the only way for my spiritual operation to be performed and for the effects of it to be manifested. I began to move into the realm of the spirit and tap into the Lord, asking for healing and asking to be used for his honor and glory. It was hard letting go of pent-up memories, but God wanted to heal me. If I hadn't released these thoughts, the job would not have been done. God is all powerful and can force us to conform but can also choose not to go against the will of man. The Almighty does not force us to release our burdens to him against our will. We have to be active participants in God's presence, and I was. I knew that it was my time to heal.

I felt a tearing away inside as if I had digested a mild trace of acid. The willingness to change is sometimes hard work. It is hard to change even those things that are not good for you. Daily, I began to feel restored and enlightened as if a weight had been lifted from me. I recalled the Scripture, "Jesus Christ is the same yesterday, today, and forever" (Hebrew 13:8, NIV). If Jesus did this for me, he would do it for anyone. Healing allows us to release grudges, hurt, bitterness, anger, and pain and to grow in the fruit of the spirit: love, joy, peace, longsuffering, temperance, goodness, gentleness, meekness and faith (Galatians 5:22). It is this level of healing that prepares us for service and functional living. I felt good and was able to even dialogue with my ex-husband without argument, a major accomplishment.

I ran into Fred on the streets of New York City over two decades after he raped me. He was now a well-respected executive in his company. He looked refined and was immaculately dressed. We chatted for a long time, updating each other like old friends. I could tell that he had developed exquisite taste for the fine amenities of life and was enjoying a level of material success. It was the American dream for him, and he flaunted it. I was already divorced, and he had never married. I remembered thinking, maybe he has changed and our meeting was a divine appointment. How wrong I was, but he could have been a mind reader because he invited me to dinner. I was leaving New York and going back to Boston the following day and had to decline. However, we agreed that he would visit me in Boston. And he did.

While in Boston, it did not take long for Fred's rapist ways to surface, and he tried to force himself upon me again. He had not changed. I got in his face and threatened to have him locked up and more. I must confess that my words got a little dirty. I soon toned down to reflect more of a Christian image but remained firm on my threat to call the police. I told him, "As a woman I will not have you or anybody else violate my body. Women are not toys." Fred said to me, "You have changed." I interpreted that to mean that I had stood up for my rights with a fearless spirit. He said, "I do not want you because you are too black for me." I wondered how black is too black and dismissed his statement as frivolous. He continued to make very insulting remarks, but I appeared unmoved by his insolence. When Fred got back to New York, he called me to continue his verbal assault. It was my turn to show some chutzpah. I took great liberty in being arrogant, sassy, and brass faced before hanging up the phone on him.

Praise Dance: An Encounter with God

It is times like the above experience that I tend to put on my leotard and exercise or dance in the privacy of my living room as a form of release. Praise dance is a language of worship unto God. It is sacred and should not be displayed as a mere performance but should be offered up to God as a sacrifice of praise and worship in thanksgiving. Miriam the Prophetess offered this level of praise. She rejoiced at the victory of the Israelites and the demise of Pharaoh as God delivered his people via the Red Sea. Exodus 15:19–20 reads,

> For the horse of Pharaoh went in with his chariots and with his horsemen into the Red Sea, and the Lord brought again the waters of the sea upon them: but the children of Israel went on dry land in the midst of the sea. And Miriam the Prophetess, the sister of Aaron, took a timbrel in her hand: and all the women went out after her with timbrels and with dances.
>
> KJV

These women must have been of all shapes, sizes, and ages, but in worship, it did not matter.

King David also knew how to minister unto God. When the Ark of the Covenant was being transported into the city of David, King David danced in worship until his clothes fell off, much to his wife Michal's embarrassment and disapproval. As the Ark of the Covenant was brought into the city of David, King David was beside himself in worship (2 Samuel 6:14–16). Psalm 149:3 is irrefutable in its instructions and does not make any gender or venue distinctions when it states, "Let them praise his name with dancing and make music to him with tambourine and harp" (Psalm 149:3, NIV).

Praise dance is worship that must be directed unto the Lord. It is an inward action that is reflected outward and upward and is not an inward action that is reflected outward and downward. In praise dance worship, I thrive to press up and tap into the presence of God as my primary goal. Tapping into the presence of God will inevitably connect with the soul of man, and the audience will benefit as a secondary recipient. The concept of a performance is slightly different since its goal is to first satisfy and connect with the audience.

A performance is still in the category of entertainment, just as blue jeans are still classified as sportswear. Worship is in the category of praise. For example, Alvin Ailey's modern dance piece called "Revelations" is a powerfully moving spiritual rendition, while it is still a performance geared to move its human audience. The American Heritage Dictionary's definition of *modern dance* is, "a style of theatrical dance that rejects the limitations of classical ballet and favors movement deriving from the expression of inner feelings."[1] Praise dance in this era tends to be rooted in, but not limited to, the style of modern dance.

In spite of the dance style, both performance and praise dance require a necessary measure of internal personal soul-searching and getting in tune with one's self to be able to express oneself in creativity and sometimes intuitiveness. Because of this a performance could often be perceived as worship. The distinction must be that praise dance displays a desire to worship, recognizing its primary purpose is to minister to God. Anything less is shifting the order, and the total effect of God's present would not be felt.

I have spoken to praise dance leaders who seem to hold the worldly view image that praise dancing is only to be tried by thin and younger women. I knew of a praise dance team that exclusively recruited thin runway model type girls, excluding the plump ones. Consequently this image, influence, and taste causes perceptions that detract from worship. Praise dance, for me, is more than a physical act. It is a spiritual deed.

It is important that any form of worship be from the heart, an offering to God. Watchman Nee, in his book *Ministering to the House or to God?* said, "What I fear most in my heart is that many will come out to preach the gospel to help men, save sinners, and perfect the believers yet not minister to the Lord." Praise dance ministers to God. When praise dance is done as unto the Lord, it moves from the outer court of praise to the inner court of worship, tapping into the realm of the holy of holies. It is at this point that intimacy with God is established. When I praise dance, I experience a sweet pure presence that is shadowed by a gentle touch from the master. My soul and the body are in total subjection to the directive of the Holy Spirit, who takes the lead. This creates a flow of oneness, the kind of electricity that supersedes everything else around. It generates a joy from the bottom of my soul.

Praise dance is one of the purest encounters that I have experienced in worship as the presence of God is ushered in. Praise dance does not necessarily have to be liturgical. A simple body sway, movement of the feet, arms, and head in worship can be categorized as praise dance. I formally started to learn dance at the age of six. I started with ballet and then moved on to contemporary dance, tap, limbo, African and Indian dance and even tried to learn belly dancing but failed at that one. I started, as a teenager, to experiment with choreographing dance. Years later, I was delighted to be asked to teach dance at an art center in Birmingham, England. This center hosted performing arts programs for middle and primary school kids.

It was there I gained confidence in my ability to choreograph and dance, and at this point that I began to incorporate dance movements with gospel music. I was so excited by the electricity that I felt as I experimented on the art form for worship that I asked my pastor to praise dance at our church concert. This request almost ignited World War Three. My pastor threatened to expel me from the church roll.

In the years to follow, I continued to dance to all different types of music in the privacy of my bedroom, living room, or bathrooms. I choreographed on the spot, with or without music, as the Holy Spirit led. I enjoyed listening and dancing to Indian music, using the sound tracts from popular Indian movies. My love for dance as an art form and dance as worship gave me a seriousness for the art. I jokingly shared with a friend that there were times when I felt that I missed my calling as a professional dancer.

The depth of my desire and experience in dance has inspired me to develop the following praise dance guidelines. The goal is to establish the distinction between dance as a performance and dance as a form of worship.

1. Understand the purpose of praise dance and make that distinction between performance and worship.

2. Don't be caught up in size, weight, gender, and age as criteria for admission to the praise dance group. The only way an age distinction should be made in praise dance is if, for example, one wants to have a children's group distinct from adults.

3. Let your actions in dance be from the heart as an act of worship. To help accomplish this, individuals must spend time preparing the heart through prayer and a simple desire to worship.

4. Musical selections as well as the choreography must be spirit led and inspired.

5. Do not seek to be perfect and flawless in your "performance," rather seek to give of your best and rely on God to do the rest. In this way, the Lord will honor your desire to worship and will take you beyond self.

6. Give God the glory and do not become conceited when you are complimented for your vigor in worship.

7. There is much validity and purpose in doing warm-up exercises before dancing, just as it's important for a singer or basketball team to do warm-ups. However, in praise dance rehearsals, the emphasis must not be solely on stretching but on praying and jelling as a team.

8. The dance team must establish oneness to be able to do corporate worship in unison. The goal is for the Holy Spirit to be allowed to freely flow to the extent that the team gets caught up in God's glory, allowing the spirit of praise to penetrate the sanctuary.

9. How do you measure your success in praise dance worship? Measure your success in worship not by how many accolades you receive but by whether you have touched heaven where the presence of God engulfs your being, catching you up in the

holy of holies where your spirit connects with your Creator.

10. Do not allow yourself to be easily deterred or distracted from worship. Examine your motives and be a self-motivated worshipper.

Once I recognized the purpose and power of praise dance, I understood why the devil tries to block this and every other form of worship. Common strategies the devil uses to sabotage worship are to bring division among worshipers and to evoke religious spirits that rely on the organization's by-laws instead of God's laws, creating the wrong emphasis and belief system.

I'll share a very funny but embarrassing experience that almost kept me glued to my seat in non-participation during praise and worship at a Calvary Church summer camp meeting in Ashland, Virginia (although it's very difficult for me to be non-participative in worship). I was praise dancing in my seat, and an old lady sitting in front of me kept looking back at me with one of those "you are a sinner" look, the look that you often get from super righteous religious fads when you go to some churches without wearing a hat. By the way, hats are never a requirement at Calvary. This old lady was wearing a beautiful lace cloth pinned to the middle of her head. I lifted my hands and stretched in a circular dance movement; my fingers got caught in the old lady's hair and tipped her wig over. Her wig and lace cloth fell to the ground. She scrambled to retrieve her false hair and quickly placed it back on her head, the wrong way.

I made haste to apologize. My daughter was fighting to contain her laughter and so were a few women in my row. I felt like a worm. The woman, by this time, was openly outraged. Both her hands started to wave in the air and I could see the movement of her lips running like a motor, but the loud music drowned out her words. I quietly took my seat as she settled down to hers. My daughter needed to go to the bathroom, and we both exited the sanctuary, rolling with laughter.

While it is healthy and customary to engage in different forms of worship, some denominations do not permit praise dance or lifting up holy hands as a form of worship, just as some denounce speaking in tongues as a manifestation from the devil. These acts are sometimes viewed as unacceptable and non-scriptural. I recall this being the case at a church that I used to attend. One Sunday morning at the end of the worship service, I was pulled aside by a deacon who told me that lifting holy hands and praise dancing was prohibited because it was not written in the church's by-laws. The deacon said that the people there were essentially uncomfortable with my form of worship. I got the message and respectfully moved on. While our attitude should not be judgmental to those who worship differently, it helps to be in a congregation that does not get freaked out by your form of worship.

Memorable Treasures

Johnson's Baby Powder Girl

As a child, I could have easily advertised for the Johnson and Johnson Company because I smelled of Johnson's baby powder well into my teenage years. In fact, I still love the scent. From the time I was a baby, my mother would flour my elder sister, Carol, and me with baby powder as if preparing us to be dropped in hot oil. My friends sometimes teased me because the powder would make a cake on my neck when I perspired in the hot Caribbean sun.

My braids always looked well starched into place but always hurt because they were too tight. I still hate to comb my hair. My mom took great pride in decorating my braids with different color satin ribbons to match my outfits. The wind would blow my ribbons loose, and I could see them fly through the air like kites in the wind. She custom made most of my clothes and was in love with putting large bows at the back of each of my dresses. My expensive, brand new Clarke's Shoes were always one size bigger than my feet and stuffed with toilet paper.

My mother's theory was simply that I would grow into them.

In these outfits, I was expected to act like a lady but I really just wanted to be like Tom Sawyer on another boyish adventure, only in the confines of my backyard. Being a girl meant acting daintily, and I just wanted to be real and be allowed the same privileges as my male cousins. No one was telling them to sit quietly when wearing their black pants and white shirts with bowties, because they were boys.

Mother as Role Model

My mom was a very creative, intelligent, and self-motivated woman. I remembered the day that she walked off her job as a store clerk. I was about six-years-old. Mummy came home mid-morning, looking sad. I knew that her mother had not died because Ma was sitting in the living room. Mummy was wearing a fitted black skirt and a white blouse with black ballerina shoes. Her skin was flawless, and her curly black hair flowed softly down her shoulders. She was a strikingly beautiful woman. Ma asked her why she was home so early, and before she answered, I was asked to go to the next room. I cracked the door so that I could listen to their conversation. My mom said that she walked off of her job because she had had enough of her boss's sexual advances. I did not know what sexual harassment was, but I was all ears. Ma said, "You are right," and asked what Mummy was going to do now. Mummy's reply stuck with me for the rest of my life and gave me a no-tolerance level for sexual harassment. She told Ma, "I will not give in like all the other girls on my job, and I will find a way to feed my children without selling my body to do it." Ma agreed. My mom found another job, first as a cashier, then as a secretary, and moved her way up to head supervisor of the accounting department during her over twenty-two years in the largest labor party on the island. She always seemed to get the job done.

In mid life, my mom resigned her job and headed up her own company for the next twenty-five years. I admired her entrepreneurial spirit. She is now retired. We often reminisce and laugh at some of her experiences and some of her parenting skills. For example, when I had my menstrual period for the first time, in my early teens, I thought that I had contracted a terminal disease. My mother's parenting skills did not help. She had two words of advice for me: I must maintain good hygiene as a young lady and stay away from boys. Oops, this raised my curiosity, but I dared not ask a question, because mother knows best.

Learning to Follow Through

My mom taught me the importance of following through on task. I had to follow through on my weekly unpaid house chores. Her lesson is a memorable treasure because I learned from an early age to see a task through to the end and be committed to completing what I have started. The discipline I developed helped me to be very productive in the secular world.

Mummy also cultivated in me a habit of saving for a rainy day. Later in life, my rainy day nest egg came in very handy. When I was a child, my mom opened a family credit union to teach my sister and me money management and money sense. I had to create a ledger of how I spent my allowance and then justify my spending to her. Mummy acted as our financial counselor. This would form the basis for discussion. I was mandated to put a portion of my allowance in this imaginary home credit union. My mother was the banker. I remembered her talking about saving through diversification of assets although she did not use these terms. She spoke about fixed deposits, personal saving accounts, investment in real estate, conservation in spending, education, and healthy eating all as forms of investment. She was right on the button. My first job was a summer assignment at my mother's office. I was thrilled to receive pay for my services and had a picture in my mind of shopping for a new outfit. But when I was given my salary, Mummy accompanied me to her company's credit union to open an account. I bought my mom and dad thank you gifts, and my first check that looked like so much money was gone and so were my chances of owning a new outfit that week.

There were times like these when I was upset by Mummy's overpowering control. As I grew older, her examples became my memorable treasures.

Booze Cupboard

I liked going to garden tea parties with my mother and sometimes enjoyed the attention when she floated me around like I was a circus horse. In fact, I was dressed for the part. She and my dad also did a fair amount of entertaining at home. My dad had a special cupboard full of booze. I would sneak into the cupboard and help myself to a drink or two. Then I would fill up the whisky bottle with water. My mom would often mix a drink for herself and my dad when they were relaxing, listening to her favorite Ray Charles album. One night, I heard my father complaining that his drink was very weak. Mummy told him that she used the same measuring glass as always. I ran back into my bedroom before they caught me eavesdropping. My mom always instilled in us that stealing is wrong, and that night I felt convicted and decided not to raid his booze cupboard again.

Pa Lookoo

My image of my grandfather's life and death is another memorable treasure. He was a very well respected man in his community, and he helped a lot of people. He was fondly known as Lookoo, and I came to be known as Lookoo's granddaughter. Even today, there are people who still call me by no other name. Pa was of Indian descent. His acquired wealth and generous giving made him an icon of sort. Our family history that was passed down through the generation goes like this: Pa Lookoo was a descendent of a very rich Indian royal family from the Eastern part of India. Truth or fiction, he played the part. But the family history is still a little fuzzy, particularly when Aunt Marjorie tells it. Pa's family name was Pudrasingh, no doubt from the Punjab area in India, perhaps from the Slik sect. We don't know how his forefather ended up as an indenture slave on the Caribbean island of Trinidad. Rumor has it that his forefather was involved with a white woman and was disbanded from the family. Pa's family name was later changed to Joseph in Trinidad to conform to the mandate of Catholicism. In those days, becoming a Catholic included having to adopt a Christian name.

Pa was always immaculately dressed and carried himself like royalty, except when he had had a few drinks and was cussing Ma behind closed doors. He had, of course concubines, two of which each bore him a child, but this was a closely guarded family secret. Even my grandmother pretended that she did not know of Pa's unfaithfulness. She was that much of a peacemaker, but had it been me in a similar situation, I would have been kicking butts, including Pa's, all the way back to India. In Trinidad the practice of a kind of polygamy is prevalent in the culture, although not legal. It is not unusual for men and sometimes women to be secretly involved with multiple sexual partners in and outside of marriage, often without the consent and knowledge of the other partner. This behavior is not characteristic of merely Caribbean culture, but cheating husband and wives can be found worldwide.

My grandfather's death when I was nine had a great impact on me. I was moved by the crowds that turned up to pay their last respects to him. It felt like he was a rock star or a king. I felt ten feet tall and knew that someday I wanted to impact lives as he did by reaching out and helping the marginalized. Pa's casket laid in state at our family's home as hundreds shuffled through in respectful silence. I remembered being afraid to look at the casket. Then it was time to go to the church for his final mass. There were no cars, just a hearse. As the procession slowly walked just under a mile to the church, another memorable experience for me was looking back from the front of the line and seeing a sea of mourners as far as my eyes could reach. My uncles had taken the coffin out of the hearse and were bearing him on their shoulders. When we got to the church, it was almost filled with mourners, some being older folks who could not make the walk. In that moment I felt special to be a part of that family and his legacy.

Battle of the Washing Machine

One victorious moment was when I won the battle of the washing machine. In anticipation of additional household chores at the birth of my first born son, Atiba, my husband and I purchased a new washing machine. It cost a couple thousand in Trinidadian dollars, and this was a significant purchase for a newly married couple. We paid in cash. A few days later, the machine stopped working. I made numerous calls to the company before they sent out a repair man. Two days later the washing machine broke down again. I requested a full refund and was ignored by the supervisor. I went back to the store and demanded to speak with the manager, but he refused to see me and subsequently did not return my calls. I was stuck with a lemon and caring for a newborn baby. I was upset and did not like the feeling of being robbed. I knew that if I had been a man, the store personnel would have shown me a little more respect. I tried to ask my husband to intervene, but I was fighting a losing battle. I could tell by his grunts that he did not have the energy or interest to fight another war after his long work days as an educator and entrepreneur and late-night shifts as a new dad. I was on my own.

As a mom turned investigator, I started my own Sherlock-Holmes-style investigation. I got two vital pieces of information; the store manager's home address and the time he got to work each morning. It turned out that he lived in my neighborhood just around the corner from my house. I estimated the time he would have to leave his house in the morning to get to work for his regular arrival time, allowing for traffic jams and other variables. I devised a plan for our meeting. Timing was important and since my baby was not yet in a sleeping and breastfeeding pattern, I ran the risk of blowing my own plan should the baby require a feeding. At daybreak I sneaked into my car, still wearing my house robe, hair uncombed and teeth not brushed. My lack of hygienic care was not a part of the plan, but it worked for convenience and timing. Off I went to park my car in front of the store manager's driveway in protest to make my demands absolutely clear. Since he refused to see me at his office, I was certain this action would get his attention and get me the required results. I was seeking either a full refund for the washing machine or a new one within twenty-four hours.

My car was a white new Mini. Its polished body glittered as the morning sun pierced through the clouds. I positioned myself at the store manager's gated entrance and waited. It was not long before his door swung open, and I could hear him bidding his wife goodbye. He turned around and saw me standing by his gate. I will never forget the look on his face as he walked down his driveway to the front gate. He looked frightened. His non-verbal expression seemed to ask, "Are you the girl from my rendezvous last night?" I set my face like Judge Judy when she wants to assert her authority. The store manager did not know me, but his wife sure thought that he did. Her facial expression was equally as comical. She seemed puzzled and charged to the gate as if to confront her husband and his concubine. He looked at her and shrugged his shoulders. I broke the silence by introducing myself, and then I began telling my story. I could see the relief on his face. He interrupted me, requesting that I move my car and meet with him at his office later that day. I ignored him and turned to his wife, continuing to state my case. She listened intensely, without interrupting me. I also apologized for any embarrassment that my presence may have caused, as by this time her neighbors were leaving for work. Some were discreetly slowing down by her gate "maccoing," a local parlance used to describe nosy people. I reiterated that this was not just all about my washing machine but about consumer rights and effecting change in her husband's business practices. I watched in amazement at what ensued next. The wife became my advocate. She commanded her husband to immediately replace my washing machine or give me a full refund. He nodded to her in silent obedience. He turned his attention to me and humbly asked that I move my car to allow him to go to work since he wanted to catch the delivery van before it left for that day's deliveries. I drove off laughing until I cried. My new washing machine arrived before noon that same day. This was a memorable treasure for me because I felt that I stood up for my rights and defended consumer rights for every other consumer.

Special Moments

The birth of each of my three children will forever be my most memorable experiences, three moments in time when it felt like all of heaven was saying to me, "You go, girl." And I did. Moments like that will never return except in a memory of lasting treasures. In each of those three moments of birth delivery, I offered my babies back to God. I vowed to raise them up according to God's will for their life by teaching them the things of God. To the best of my ability, I have.

Memorable Movie

I used to like watching John Wayne's cowboy movies and other old films like the 1959 *The World, the Flesh, and the Devil* by Harry Belafonte. In this movie, Belafonte plays the role of a miner who gets trapped when the cave that he is working in collapses. He digs himself out only to discover that the world was destroyed by a nuclear catastrophe and he seemed to be the sole survivor of mankind. He manages to make his way from Philadelphia to New York City and discovers two other survivors: a young white man and a beautiful, twenty-two-year-old white woman.

Belafonte's character reminded me of the family movie, *Land before Time.* Two dinosaurs, a short tail and a long neck, are separated from their herd by a catastrophic volcanic eruption. Facing extinction, they find each other. The short tail was maintaining his species rank and status quo when he refused to play with the long neck. He told him, "Short tails don't play with long necks."

Similarly, in *The World, the Flesh, and the Devil,* Belafonte wouldn't kiss the white woman. I had a hard time understanding why such a macho man wouldn't give in to her. She demanded that he make love to her, and he did not budge. I later understood that this movie depicted a historical account of the race barriers in America during that period of time. Belafonte bluntly refused to have sex with the only woman left alive on planet Earth because he was a "Negro." He pussyfooted around her advances throughout the movie, suppressed his desire to have her, even hesitating to even hold her hand in the ending scene all because he was afraid of the repercussions of a black man being sexually involved with a white woman. His actions were a reflection of racial tension in society in that era. In movie land today, actor Will Smith would not have hesitated to go all the way with that white woman, with remorse.

While in movie-land race relations have changed drastically, and to some extent one can say race relations have improved in America, we still have much work to do in bridging the gap. Over the years, I have admired Belafonte's pioneer work on race and humanitarian issues as he helped to showcase and remedy injustice.

Where Are My Spoils?

Lessons

The Webster dictionary defines *spoils* as, "prizes won or treasures accumulated."[2] But winning is no easy task, and it always comes with a price paid in battle. Some of my battles in life have been intense, and there were many times when I wanted to roll over and play dead and surface after the storm. For example, there was a period in my life when I was in a bad relationship. I kept going around in circles each time saying, "Haven't I been here before?" and thinking I did not learn the last time around. It was a clear dead end with this brother and, I knew it, but chose to grasp onto straws. He told the same lies for ten years, and I believed him for ten years. The irony of it was that I would not normally allow myself to sink into anything that is counterproductive to my wellbeing. But in this case, I was madly in love and blindly stupid. Finally, a light bulb went off in my head, and I knew that I had to do something. The former prime minister of England, Margaret Thatcher once said, "You may have to fight a battle more than once to win it."[3] Her statement for her nation's success was my approach to winning the final rounds of a bad relationship. It was, in fact, easier than I thought. I did not need to fight this battle more than once. The simple remedy was to just walk away. But I needed inner strength and moral support to be able to let go. I sought wise counsel from a few older Christian women and a male father figure, whom I trusted. Their personal shared experiences and prayers gave me the fighting zeal to walk away. I ended that relationship and felt like a newborn butterfly, light and free. The experience convinced me to reinforce my belief system, cultivating only functional relationships. Since then, I have been able to counsel others in similar predicaments.

Now, I take inventory of my personal battles and lessons learned. I always fight to win while recognizing that some battles will be lost. However, even in my lost battles, I still feel like a winner because I use the lessons to effect positive change in my life. I have observed that looking at my trials through these lenses has increased my faith in the Lord and gives me the strength to get up when I fall. As a result, I was able to stay clear of taking prescription drugs to help me navigate life's battles. To this, my daughter Nzinga jokingly teased me and said, "Mummy, you manage to stay sane while you set everybody else crazy."

There are times, just prior to a battle intensifying in my life, when I dream about these battles and sometimes feel spiritual attacks in my dreams. In these dreams, I am confronted with evil attacks, and I often pray until deliverance comes. Dreams and visions have always fascinated and sometimes frightened me. My interest in dreams started when I was growing up. My uncles Hilton and Harold would jokingly discuss their dreams, and Harold would solicit from the family accounts of their dreams. Uncle Harold was disabled at the age of sixteen by polio, which left him unable to speak, but he had a positive spirit that inspired me. His work ethic was admirable. He never missed a day as a handy man and janitor in the ship repair company called Tugs and Lighters. He was convinced that dreams gave him the winning tips for bets on an illegal game called "Way-Way," which was secretly played by many of the old timers. The rules of this game were never discussed, and I never found out how it worked.

Way-Way was his sport of choice. We always knew when the Way-Way "mark bust," a term they used when a winner was declared. If Harold won, he would make a humorous sound like a turkey and do a victory dance. Joy lit up his face, and spit trickled down his chin, forming an elastic line which never seemed to bother him. He was independent and gutsy in an era when the disabled had no place in society. I admired how he found ways to entertain and support himself. Harold's excitement about dreams ignited me to pay special attention to my dreams. Not simply for the purpose of getting winning Way Way tips but to determine, in a spiritual sense, which of my dreams to dismiss as a result of overeating and which were specific warnings that required my prayerful attention.

Some dreams have proven beneficial in helping me to make the decision to draw closer to God.

In one such dream, I found myself walking in a densely populated area. This dream motivated me to get my Christian life back on track with the Lord. In the dream, the scenery looked like the streets of Manhattan in the movie *The Muppets Take Manhattan.* I felt like Kermit the Frog navigating the streets in style and confidence. Suddenly and without any effort, I started to slip and slide on an invisible sheet of black ice. My leg got caught in a crack on the sidewalk, and I started to plunge below. I felt sucked in, and in a flash realized that I was going underground level into the earth, fighting to maintain my balance but to no avail. When I stopped falling, I found myself submerged in the depth of the sea, but I was breathing without the help of an oxygen tank. I was out of the comfort of my safety zone looking in at my world as an outsider or from the outside.

Violently I waved my hands, beckoning for help. No one was looking down, and no one else was falling in. My desperate shouts for help from deep under sea went unnoticed. My efforts only created large and small bubbles of air. I felt trapped and helpless. Turning to the Lord, I started to pray. I dreamed this at a point in my life's journey when, at a professional level, I was experiencing success but at a personal level things were crumbling. I felt empty and devastated from another failed marriage, exposed and vulnerable with a feeling of being out on a limb with no place to hide. I found solace in this dream when I heard the voice of God say to me, "Praise me."

The voice said, "I can hear you from wherever you are, if you are on the mountain top, I am there. In the depth of the sea, I am there. Just praise me." The voice said, "Seek me and praise me from the depth of the earth. I will hear you." I heard the words of Psalms 139: 8–10 being recited to me: "If I ascend up into heaven, thou art there: if I make my bed in hell, behold, thou art there. If I take the wings of the morning, and dwell in the uttermost parts of the sea; Even there shall thy hand lead me, and thy right hand shall hold me" (KJV). I knew then that there was hope.

I awoke trembling and burst into tears. I reached for the telephone and, still weeping, I dialed my prayer partner, Dorothy. She did not ask any question but began to pray as I sobbed. Then, like a written script, Dorothy began to recite Psalms 139: 8–10 "If I ascend up into heaven, thou art there: if I make my bed in hell, behold, thou art there. If I take the wings of the morning, and dwell in the uttermost parts of the sea; Even there shall thy hand lead me, and thy right hand shall hold me" (KJV). She said, "Amen," asked if I was okay, and then she hung up. I lay on my bed, shivering like someone exposed to sub-zero temperatures without winter gear. This dream was not my gateway tip to winning a Way Way but my wake up call to reflect on my life and my relationship with the Lord.

I first recommitted to making Jesus the number one priority in my life, allowing my prayer life to reflect the same. Secondly, I volunteered time to work at church and became more involved in church activities. My plan was to seek the Lord in prayer at five every morning and let that set the pace in my life. Fifteen years have passed, and I am still on that regimen of early morning prayers and periodic fasting. One of my greatest accomplishments was learning to pray using the Word of God. Often I would quote a Scripture and then pray that Scripture, realizing many answered prayers over time.

The Prayer

I had three family deaths in less than six months. My father, stepfather, and uncle died at a time when I was experiencing some personal turbulence in my life. I lost the three men in my life, and it was devastating. I needed the Comforter. The Holy Spirit comforted me with these words:

> But I would not have you to be ignorant, brethren, concerning them which are asleep, that ye sorrow not, even as others which have no hope. For if we believe that Jesus died and rose again, even so them also which sleep in Jesus will God bring with him. For this we say unto you by the words of the Lord, that we which are alive and remain unto the coming of the Lord shall not prevent them which are asleep. For the Lord himself shall descend from heaven with a shout, with the voice of the archangel, and with the trump of God: and the dead in Christ shall rise first: Then we which are alive and remain shall be caught up together with

> them in the clouds, to meet the Lord in the air: and so shall we ever be with the Lord. Wherefore comfort one another with these words.
>
> i Thessalonians 4:13–18 (KJV)

I felt comforted by these words as I wrote my dad's eulogy, reflecting not just on his legacy, but my own. Asking and answering myself, how would I like to be remembered? First as a worshipper who selflessly obeyed God. I sat on the bed, weeping, broken, and grieved and prayed this personal prayer which I have daily prayed ever since:

My Personal Prayer

Cleanse, purify, and refine me.

I pray that my love for you will never wax cold

Let your word be verified in me, Lord, and teach me to wait on you.

God, I want to walk in your ordained plan for my life.

Holy Spirit, help me to develop the fruit of the spirit as is written in Galatians 5:22: love, joy, peace, long-suffering, gentleness, goodness, faith, meekness, and temperance, for against this there is no law.

Help me, Lord; incline my ear to wisdom and my heart to understanding.

Establish my ways.

God, I repent; forgive me and my children of our sins

Prepare me to be a sanctuary for you

Lord Jesus, preserve my way and help me to preserve my soul.

God, I pray that life be unto my soul, have mercy upon me, oh Lord.

God, open to me the gates of righteousness.

Help me, Lord, to cease the moment of my season.

God, forgive me for debt and free me from the captivity of debt.

Open to me the windows of heaven and pour out a blessing on my seed.

Hide the word of God in my heart, so I will not sin against you.

I pray in Jesus' name, Amen.

I began to declare and denounce things in my life and radically seek the Lord's approval for every step that I took. This prayer and approach took root in my spirit. It felt like a potent weed killer had finally saturated the reoccurring weed that killed the beautiful rose plant before it could even bud.

Wholeness began to take over my very being. An alignment of soul, body, and spirit jelled as the dross of sadness, emptiness, and bitterness peeled away. In its place grew more compassion, greater wisdom, understanding, and strength. It was a struggle to maintain my newfound position because of my reoccurring insecurities and hurts. There was a war going on inside of me to actually release that which was counterproductive to my wellbeing. I read

Galatians 5:17, "For the flesh lusteth against the Spirit, and the Spirit against the flesh: and these are contrary the one to the other: so that ye cannot do the things that ye would" (KJV). This Scripture was a tremendous revelation that helped me in dealing with spiritual warfare. I learned not to entertain the spirit of doubt, fear, and negativity but to maintain a positive, bold spirit knowing that, "I can do all things through Christ who strengthens me" (Philippians 4:13, NKJV). I knew then that I was healed from the pain of loss and my inner turbulence. My joy had returned, never again allowing life's challenges and trials to steal my joy. I have learned that praying without ceasing is the key to deliverance and answered prayer.

The deeper I got into a disciplined prayer life and an understanding of the Word of God, the lonelier my spiritual walk became. I had to shake off some friends and family, even Christian friends who could not see where God wanted to take me. They blocked my path by drawing me into more church projects and good deeds and by constantly reminding me of the security of a risk free life. I say a risk free life is a faithless life. A few of my secular friends may have thought that I needed my head checked since I had lost my taste for socializing in favor of spending the time reading my Bible. The separation did me well, and as I felt more grounded in the Word of God, I was able to revisit some of my acquaintances with a new message of the goodness of Jesus.

It is important for me to continually draw on the mercy of the Lord to keep going and growing. "It is of the Lord's mercies that we are not consumed, because his compassions fail not. They are new every morning: great is thy faithfulness." (Lamentations 3:22-23, KJV). I was very grateful to the Lord Jesus Christ for the compassion shown to me and the strength that I drew through the mercies of God.

I started the practice of fasting when I was twelve-years-old. When I was a child, my grandmother fasted and prayed a lot, and my mother had developed a disciplined life of fasting and praying. Fasting became an integral part of my life. I practiced both strict and partial fasts for one, three or twenty-one days. Many days, I would have just one meal and go weeks on only water, juices, fruits, and vegetables. There were three-day periods without food or water. One year, after a twenty-one day combination of strict and partial fasting, I felt led into a forty-day partial fast later that same year. When that fast ended, I cautiously continued fasting regularly for the next eighteen months, consistently praying and seeking God's will for my life on each fast. I became aware of a cycle of body changes during my fasting period. Some days in the early stages of the fast, I would get a headache and feel very hungry. Then, after a few days, I would not feel hungry at all but irritable and deep in the darkness of frustration before I would feel the light of breakthrough. There were cycles in my fasting when at times it felt like all of hell was on my door step. I experienced deep periods of spiritual attacks and heaviness. I was fighting battles even in my dreams. These symptoms, I have been told, are not unusual in an extended fast. My key was to always combine fasting with prayer, and my mother always told me that any fast must be spirit led.

During one such extended fast, I experienced lingering irritability, weakness, and felt withdrawn. Fearing depression of some sort, I went to see my doctor. He assured me that I was not depressed, but suggested that I break the fast. My blood count was good, and my mind intact. I was not mad. Halleluiah, if only my ex-husband could have gotten that revelation. The doctor strongly recommended that I eat and rest and "get a life," which he defined as dating. I evoked my Fifth Amendment right to silence and did not comment, but I left his office laughing and thinking to myself, *This doctor is earning over one hundred thousand dollars a year. He could afford to rest.* In fact, he looked like the one needing to "get a life." Nevertheless, it was refreshing to think that I was not going mad. Numerous times I wanted to stop fasting, eat everything in sight, and follow doctor's orders. My key was to always combine fasting with prayer, a practice that helped me to stand my ground and draw strength in spiritual battle to overcome tests and trials with God's grace. Now I was ready to receive my spoils as a tangible inheritance from God.

Where Are My Spoils?

I was a productive citizen, who strived to keep myself holy by example, including: years of sexual abstinence and living a life of Christian principles with integrity and character. I have had many questions asked of me about my sexual abstinence, but never felt that I had to defend this position. However, for my curious readers, I am not "cold," anti-sex, or a man hater. In fact, I am quite the opposite. But I understand that God does not approve of sex outside of marriage. Sex is sacred, so there is no more playing around for me. Life is still filled with personal challenges for me, but during my last inventory, I was doing well as a front runner. I gave myself an A grade on my imaginary report card.

I erroneously thought that as a result of my good behavior, hard work, and personal victories that financial wealth and opportunities would be running me down just begging me to take them. But, where are my spoils? God must have commanded a blessing on me. In my ignorance, I expected that the apple pie I ate yesterday would still be in the sky for another taking today. And, of course, after all those years without sex, the shining knight would be perched high on his horse outside of my window, ready to propose marriage. Instead, the heavens were silent. My school loan and bills were still to be paid, the apple pie was already digested and gone, and most of all, the knight nowhere in sight. "What's up, Lord? Did I miss my spoils?" No, but I needed to put life in perspective. Under all the fasting and praying, I simply needed to understand that the Lord should not be treated as my sugar daddy or investment broker. My Lord and Savior Jesus Christ must be treated with reverence. I realized that my motives for serving had to be right, and that spoils, although tangible, are often also intangible, though measurable. For example, the spiritual growth one derives from exercising one's faith and as a result being able to look back, with strength, at how one successfully overcame a problem or challenge.

I had tapped into God's perfect will for my life without even knowing it. I already understood that the primary purpose for God creating me was to worship the Lord. What, then, was my secondary purpose? I heard the voice of God speaking to me saying, "I am using you as a bridge to connect my people to my resources and to connect my people to me." A renewed fire kindled in my spirit. I had heard these words a decade before, from a friend in Cambridge, Massachusetts—Pastor Larry Ward, a then rookie pastor who inherited a thriving ministry from his father. I had worked closely with Pastor Larry on areas of church growth and development and strategies for taking his ministry outside of the confines of its eighty-year-old walls. After one of our very successful community outreach events, Pastor Larry looked me in the eye and randomly said, "You are a connector. That's your calling. Your gift is bringing people together and you know how to access resources." I laughingly took the compliment but did not run with it as a "calling." However, over the years, my comfort level, satisfaction, and passion has been volunteering to work closely with inner-city churches on program development, administration, policy and planning, grant research, and elderly care issues.

One such paid assignment was to do an analysis of a faith-based organization that was eighty-five-years old. The goal was to advance recommendations, to make a case for the central office to return to Cambridge (its original base) and to develop a campaign program to elect its assistant president to the office of president at the upcoming general assembly. At the end of the process, all these goals were accomplished, and I was amazed at the level and intensity of political campaigning that was necessary. It was an eye opener to see the church involved in the same competitive political tactics as a candidate running for state representative. However, it was an honor to be able to work with members of clergy. These men and women all had a commitment to their "calling." That made me curious. Each of them seemed to have helped me in my spiritual walk with God, and some even challenged me to, "take the next step."

Tent Crusades

That next step in my spiritual journey came when a female pastor who started a church that was fifteen-years-old wanted to develop a plan for community outreach. Her church was located in the inner-city of Cambridge, Massachusetts in an area called Area IV, where there was a high concentration of low-income families, crime, unemployment, and immigrants of all different nationalities, dialects, and languages.

Pastor Nerissa suggested an outdoor crusade. I suggested community canvassing and hosting community-based events, for example, a get-to-know-your-community family day in the church's parking lot. I had already done research on Area IV for another project and was familiar with its demographic. I knew the community's challenges and was able to readily identify issues. I had served on an independent school board in this area and was a board member of a non-profit organization located in the area, which provided some social services, a vibrant after-school program, and a food pantry. I had friends who lived in Area IV.

The church set out to do its first annual tent crusades. A primary challenge in hosting these outdoor events was to obtain city permits. My job was to navigate this task. I was, at that time, the co-chair of the City of Cambridge Substance Abuse Task Force, a position that afforded me an understanding of the system. It was no picnic trying to navigate the city's bureaucracy, but we got the necessary permits. Our second challenge was literally a lack of manpower. We did not have enough men in the church to help set up and guard the tent. Sister Kathleen, armed with her ugly Pit Bull, worked the night shifts, and a number of us floated for the day shifts. We had to guard everything from the light bulbs to the musical equipment and chairs from being stolen by drug addicts.

In theory the plan was to always have two persons for each shift. In practice, we did not have enough manpower. I found myself in a shift in the middle of the day alone on duty. It was lonely, and I was uncomfortable—more like scared stiff. I saw three young boys approaching, and I ducked down behind the drum set to hide, hoping that they would just keep on going. I froze when they made a turn to come inside of the tent and started to rummage through the bags of food. I knew that it would not be long again before they discovered me perched behind the drum set. My mind was racing for a plan, so I made a decision to pop up and scare them. These boys were far from being scared; in fact they were amused. I raced through my thoughts for a Plan B. I composed myself and stood upright like a fearless warrior and offered them some food. The boys were hysterically laughing, so I nervously laughed as well and walked toward them, boldly encroaching on their space. The eldest of the three appeared to be the leader. He replied, "We do not want food." That was my gateway into conversation. When I asked why, he said, "We ain't hungry." I said, "I am always hungry for cookies," reaching into the bag of cookies and biting into a chocolate cookie. I hate chocolate. The boys were staring at me as if to ask, "Is she all right?" I had another cookie, asking them if they were sure that they were not hungry. They looked at each other in silence. I quickly asked the little one, "How old are you?" The question broke the ice. He said, "Nine, and he is eleven," pointing at the ringleader. I said, "I have two sons just like you, and I remember when they were nine and eleven." I asked the other, "And how old are you?" He said, "Ten." Now I was getting somewhere. The three boys had each spoken.

We talked for over two hours about living in the projects, the drug addicts that smoked crack cocaine on their back steps, their single mothers, and about neighborhood happenings. I was getting firsthand information on the urban poor. This was a door opening for ministry even before the official start of the crusade. The ten-year-old boy told me that he did not care about life because there was no future in the ghetto and that he would not live to reach eleven. The older one tried to stop him from talking, but he opened up and said that every night something comes into his bedroom and tells him that he must kill himself before reaching age eleven. With conviction he ended, "I'll do it; there is nothing out here to live for." To my amazement his nine-year-old brother looked at him and exclaimed, "Me, too! It always comes into my room to tell me to kill myself." "What does it look like?" I asked. The older boy said, "I don't know; but at nights I feel like someone is in my room, and then my thoughts tell me to kill myself." "Where is your mom?" I asked. He replied, "She goes out at nights." Their friend jumped in the conversation and said, "I always feel like killing myself when I am alone, and one day I will do it." I became overwhelmed with compassion, and my heart as a mother was filled. I wanted to just hug those young men and assure them of the possibility of a better life. I wanted to visit their home and try to connect their mother with city services, but the boys did not share their addresses with me for fear of the police coming to their house. In the course of conversation, one boy said that a Christian man used to stop by and talk with his mother and take him to church but that the man had stopped coming. In less than a minute, the man walked by the tent, and the little boy hailed him. I spoke with this man, who said he was a pastor and would follow up with the family, but he refused to give me their address because of fear of drug retaliation. I prayed for the boys and that day led all three of them to Christ. I never saw them again, but their stories made an impression on my mind, and now, many years later, I still pray for these boys. The crusades shook that community, and I was humbled to be a part of the process.

Souls Won

I continued to evangelize in Area IV and for the next four years did street ministry in Cambridge, including Harvard Square. Daily I developed a deeper unction to win souls. In my first three months of street ministry, the Holy Spirit used me to lead thirty-six people to Christ. About seventy percent of them were backsliders. Over the years I began to notice my strength in ministry was ministering to those who knew the gospel and turned away from it (backsliders). I also observed that my years of work as a community volunteer started to interlock with my new role as a lay minister. There was much overlapping and switching of my hats. For example, I volunteered to work at two food pantries, my church and a non-profit community based social service organization, distributing bags of food to the needy, and engaging them in conversation. Often I had the opportunity of praying on the spot for many, and quite a few received Jesus Christ as their Lord and Savior. Or I would speak to a jobless father on the street, and, in the process of helping him to access services, I would offer him the free gift of salvation.

Volunteerism

The plight of the urban poor pained my heart. Issues that are not only limited to the inner-city of poverty, access, drugs, homelessness, crime, and the frequency of domestic violence haunted my mind. I wanted to do more. I volunteered with community-based organizations to help the marginalized in Boston and Cambridge, Massachusetts. I volunteered as a tutor in the Cambridge adult literacy program. I counseled college-bound youth and worked on social issues. I served hot lunches at Thanksgiving time to the homeless and elderly in Boston and Cambridge and worked all year round at food pantries that distributed free food to the poor. I often would take Nzinga, my nine-year-old daughter, along with me because I wanted her to get a sense of service to the community. One of my sons, Kashaka, was volunteering at a homeless shelter, and Atiba, my older boy, got involved with a city-based substance prevention program for students. There, he was instrumental in designing outreach material on drug prevention and helping to set up forums. My family became a family of volunteers. I was a single parent dealing with my own personal challenges, but I wanted to make a difference and contribute to society. In the process, I wanted to teach my own children to give of themselves with a good citizen's spirit. My efforts were recognized with awards and citations from the city of Boston, the city of Cambridge, the State House, community groups, churches, and women's organizations. But there was no reward more gratifying than to see a single parent sign up and complete a GED course and mainstream herself into society or having a first generation college-bound young black man walk up to me on the street and say, "Thank you, Miss Dianne. I got into college." I was convinced that one person could make a difference, and I gave of myself without regrets.

No Place to Hide

Sometimes I wonder how a little island girl like me went from climbing mountains in the hills of Dibe, Trinidad, to hustling through the halls of the Massachusetts State House, files in hand. How did I go from clutching my mother's dress as she showcased me at social functions to boldly standing at a podium in a crowded room, proclaiming the Gospel of Jesus Christ? And how did I go from playing with my baldheaded doll, Teardrops, and my imaginary friends to teaching at a university in Massachusetts? The answer is I desired to succeed since I was a child, to take myself from beyond where I was to where I should be (although I did not know where I should be). I never feared the unknown, but trusted the Lord every step of the way. In my heart, I was determined never to settle for less and was certain that I would find more if I moved beyond where I was. This single thought was the primary motivating factor that transported me from the known into the unknown.

On faith I took a sabbatical and eventually left my secured government job, in the West Indies, to adopt a host culture in a far off land called the United States of America in the hope of accessing higher education and escaping a mutual divorce. I wanted to start all over again. My brother, Vaughn (deceased), had served as a United States solider in Vietnam and had once said to me, "America is the great land of opportunities." Now here I was feeling ready for the challenge but instead, I found myself out on a limb with no place to hide, having to face a new culture, different types of foods, and new people. I had no friends. This sounds like a mixture for a Molotov cocktail. There were many times when I questioned myself. Had I actually taken a step backwards when I left the Caribbean for this great American dream? It sure felt like it.

I thought I knew what would work for me in America. Upon migrating to the Boston area, my goals and mindset were pretty sound. I knew what I wanted out of life. One goal was to access higher education, and I had some ideas of how to access it. However, my knowledge, frame of reference, and sometimes passive aggressive nature did not shield me from experiencing culture shock and racism in America. In many ways, I was a naive island girl in a big city. I had been sheltered by my parents and then by my husband. Prior to migrating to the USA, I had never rented a house or lived on my own, did not frequently use public transportation, and had never experienced a night out at a bar with the girls.

In Trinidad, we had been conditioned from kindergarten to respect the teacher as the giver of knowledge. The student's role was primarily to receive and recall rather than to contribute information. I had never experienced life in a United States college classroom, in which the role of teacher is often that of a facilitator and expert, where students are encouraged to engage in class dialogue and where student opinion is heard and sometimes valued. This may seem insignificant but was quite intimidating and challenging to a newcomer. The perception of both peers and educators was that if you do not speak up, you are not smart or you may not understand what is being taught. I had to make some personal adjustments.

I remember one classroom experience in America. I began to actively participate in classroom discussion and was quite well versed on some of the issues discussed. Anytime I talked, two students would stare at me with dumb looks on their faces and then laugh. My British-flavored Trinidadian accent was too much for them to handle. They had a mix of culture shock and ignorance; one might say. One student commented that foreigners should all have to change their accent to sound more like Americans. He never defined which Americans, the ones in Boston, Alabama, or Ohio or the "Republic of Cambridge, Massachusetts," where I lived. I too, was suffering from culture shock because I expected less ignorance, particularly in an academic institution. It is a good thing that I was confident enough to continue participating in class and was not easily silenced. I was already outside of the box and would not allow anybody to put me back in. While some days were hard, I never regretted migrating. My true regret would have been to grow old wondering what life would have been like in America.

Another significant cultural change for me was to remember to make eye contact when speaking. In Trinidad, I was not taught to make eye contact when speaking to others, particularly when speaking to a teacher or an adult. Eye contact was interpreted as being rude and discourteous, but in America the lack of making eye contact is perceived as shiftiness. It was a big transition for me to unlearn a habit and to cultivate this new one.

There have been many times since when I felt dangerously exposed and out on a limb. For example, when I made the decision to write this book and realized the extent of the undertaking in terms of time and cost. I would not have had the money to pay my bills if I cut back on my consultant job to write a book. I did not have a husband or significant other to carry the financial load, and the more I thought about it is the more impossible the situation seemed. I was in a real predicament. It looked like the only way I could write my memoir was to wait until I retired and hope that I would have the concentration level and health to sit and reflect. This thought was too risky for me. It had to be now or never. I thought about how many of my clients owed me money and how much work I was doing for free. I provided consulting to small businesses, including the faith-based community doing workshops, grant research, market research, program development, and vision planning. It was time for me to do something for me. It was then that I got serious about completing this book. When clients did not pay, I sometimes had to juggle my bills, and I figured I might as well write my book and juggle for me.

I had a lot of other challenges before me as a single woman. I was continually challenged to make choices, being careful not to compromise my integrity, character, values, and morals. For example, my roommate continually invited me out for a night on the town with the girls. I did not quite know what that meant and did not bother to ask, because I just did not like the tone of her invitation. After months of refusing her, a mutual friend of ours was celebrating her birthday so we agreed to go to a club in Cambridge to celebrate. Unknown to me, the girls had set me up with a blind date. He was a short man with a rocket-shaped head whose breath had the distinct odor of sardines. When we got to the club, both girls met their dates and paired off. It took me awhile to figure out that sardine breath was mine for the night, and the thought aggravated me. I felt humiliated and insulted, but, to my friends, it was a kind gesture. I realized I was experiencing some cultural differences and, against my better judgment, accepted an invitation to dance with the gentleman. He may have prejudged me based on my roommate's fast moving lifestyle. In a matter of seconds, I felt warm sardine breath blowing in my ears. He must have had to stand on tiptoe to reach my ear. In true karate style, with a quick hand and leg movement, I shoved him off and walked back to my seat. He stood staring at me in a daze. My only goal was to get out of there as fast as I could. Missile head apologized and commended me for being different. I never saw him again after that night and never did get his name.

Boston winters are like no other. Some days it just gets cold to the bone, and being far away from home without family and few new acquaintances, cold to the bone feels like the kiss of death. I knew that to survive, I had to develop a mindset of endurance, constantly projecting my thoughts into the future by seeing the fulfillment of my goals—to access higher education for myself and my children and tap into the American dream. I thought to myself, if the Polish, the Irish, and the pilgrims made it in Boston, then I could, too. So, on those frigid winter snow days, I settled down to a hot cup of apple cider with a slice of fresh lemon and my favorite cheesecake and read a book. I have since developed an appreciation for all four seasons.

Dry Days

A friend once said to me, "If every day was a dry day, then life would be a desert." This sobering thought helped me to ponder on the reality of risk taking in my life and gave me a mindset of dealing with my mountains and valleys. To be able to view my life's journey through the lens of my friend's statement has helped me to live a life of no regrets. My trials were equally as important as my victories, and in the end both blessed me by contributing to my maturity.

One of my most irritating experiences was working with incompetent people was that they were more like square pegs in a round hole. I met a few that fit this description at my first job in Trinidad, where the government is the largest employer.

The ruling political party of thirty years ago appeared to often give campaign supporters key job positions as political payoffs, just to say thank you. It happens all over the world, nothing new under the sun. These handpicked employees wasted no time in creating a structure of cronyism. Promotion and survival in such a setting was subjected to how well one could suck up to incompetent supervisors and make them look like they were doing a great job. The buzz whenever a new employee came on board was which political leader he or she was associated with, and, depending on the rank of the political leader, employees would figuratively do a kind of crab dance around the new employee looking for favor. I never found it necessary to go this way, maybe because I had my own political security blanket through the direct contact and favor that my family already traditionally enjoyed.

Networking

While employed with the Trinidad and Tobago Government, I balanced my life with attending art exhibits and local plays and supporting efforts to voice the need for a Down Syndrome Association. Change finally came as a result of a change in the political party in which there was a political interest in the plight of the disabled and the urban poor. The grandchild of a new member of parliament had Down Syndrome, and he readily identified with the cause, vigorously advocating change at a governmental level. It was rewarding to see this cause being given significant attention and the changes that followed. It was a big breakthrough for two of my very vocal friends who were both caring for Down Syndrome kids and many others who silently waited in the background to see change.

My love for the arts grew, and my passion for helping the artist grew even more. I began to see a common trait among some local artists in their inability to market their work by often not giving themselves credit for their excellent quality of art work. My husband, a mathematics teacher, enjoyed drawing and painting. His preferred medium was using acrylic on canvas, although occasionally he used oil paint or pencil and did etchings. I turned his hobby into a marketable business. At first he said that my idea would not work, so I cut a deal with him. In lieu of spending money to buy me birthday and Christmas gifts and instead of buying me roses, I asked him to paint me something on canvas. Soon I learned how to prime the canvas and get it ready for him although I never developed my own talent to draw and paint. I made a self study of famous artists like Picasso and carefully examined the style and technique of local Caribbean artists. We made friends with many other artists. My husband migrated to England on a government teacher's exchange appointment just about the time that I was developing ideas for his first one-man art exhibit to showcase my cherished love gifts. He told me that it was impossible to stage a first one-man art exhibit without the artist. I hate the word impossible. Everybody around me told me that it could not be done except for one woman named Clara Rosa De Lima. She owned the most prominent art studio on the island. She and Stella, her business partner, were the only two women in the business. She agreed that I should host my husband's first one-man art exhibit at her studio on consignment. She was prepared to use her client base as the invitation list. Clara Rosa encouraged me to tap into the business. She helped me to bring out a lot of social skills and graces that I was taught as a child and taught me the marketing aspects of the business. She even gave me my first winter coat in anticipation of my joining my husband in England after the success of his first one-man art show.

My challenge was to convince my husband that this would work. With Clara and Stella on board, he began to feel a little more confident. However, I still had a great challenge before me. I had to create my own invitation list to add to Clara's and generate interest and public awareness among the not so avid art show attendees. I had to continually keep my husband motivated to paint in a long-distance relationship. I told him I missed him and needing a gift (his art work) to cheer me up. The paintings started to flow, one piece at a time. Clara was taking count.

The next step was to approach the local television station for publicity for the upcoming show. After many calls, I received a return call from the host of the program. Surprisingly enough, she was familiar with my husband's work because Clara Rosa had already acquired a few pieces on consignment, and this woman frequented Clara's studio. I was featured for half an hour on a television art and culture show, talking about the upcoming one-man exhibition and giving the audience a sneak preview. Being well briefed by Clara Rosa, I was amazed at how well I conversed on style, technique, brush strokes, the mediums used, and even about my upcoming trip to England. In some ways, the show was turned into the romance of long distance love. I would have hated for any of those viewers to see us years later in the divorce courts.

Next, I reached out to fellow artists in our social circles for their support. I bounced ideas off of Pat Chufoone, my neighbor and a local sculptor. My husband's friends and fellow artists Norris Iton, Harris, and Vocrossen encouraged me to keep on going. Clara's network was great. She introduced me to renowned artist Boscoe Holder, whose name was a household word. He knew my husband and was readily supportive. I remember being overwhelmed by Boscoe's authoritative voice, overpowering height, and his sound fatherly advice. I thought about the extent of my undertaking, and that's the only time that doubt entered into my spirit. Maybe I bit off a little too much too soon. But, my excitement and fearless determination quickly superseded any doubt. Another established artist named Leroy Clarke was hosting his one-man exhibit called Dwarfs and Dujwens. I attended his exhibit with my mom and dad and was pleasantly surprised when Leroy and my dad greeted each other. They had attended the same school and were boyhood friends. My networking skill was being sharpened as I quickly invited Mr. Clarke to the exhibit. I was on a roll; so next, I contacted my dance instructor and local icon, Molly Ahee, and she attended the opening night.

November 1979 was my husband's first one-man exhibition staged in his absence. The response was remarkable. It ran for two weeks, but on the opening night, the red dots placed beside the painting signified that a purchase was made. At the end of that cocktail evening, most of the paintings were sold. The following day a story was carried in the local newspapers. This experience showed me the benefits of networking. I did not know until I came to America that there was a name for what I was doing, "networking." The important thing was that now I knew how to do it. There is, however, a slightly different concept in the way I network. For example, at a social event, a person networking the room would most likely target the person or persons he or she wants to meet and often waste no time on others in the room. I like meeting people and do feel that each person is special and unique. I do not push to get in the face of only those whom I feel could help me and ignore everybody else as unimportant. Networking, for me, is giving as much as it is receiving.

I also found networking to be useful when I lived in England. My husband and I mounted art exhibits for local artists. One such exhibit showcased a piece of my work in Batik. It was my first and last display, and the first piece to sell on opening night. I felt it best to concentrate my talents on marketing.

Upon our return to Trinidad, I continued to market original art works as my second job. The only problem, and a good one, was in this secondary profession, as an art dealer, I was generating more money in one week, sometime in one day than what I labored for in one month working for the government. I was often tempted to resign but enjoyed the comfort of job security and the opportunity to be able to help others. I cherished both experiences.

Navigating Single Parenthood

In the Caribbean creating a support base was relatively easy to do because of the presence of the extended family. In America, the task was much greater in the absence of that support base, and my task was compounded by being a single parent. I had to create some sort of mechanism to help me cope with being a full-time student and mother with a full time job. I could not have done it without the strength of "my village"—the church.

My boys were now teenagers, and, in the absence of their dad, living in another state, I needed to find them positive male role models. The goal was not to replace their dad, but for them to draw from a positive black male the character of a man, in ways that I as a female could not express. For example, one of my sons was interested in becoming a lawyer. Both my girlfriend Shelby and her husband were practicing lawyers in Boston, and at that time they had no children. Shelbey agreed for her husband, David, to mentor my son, Kashaka. The chemistry between David and Kashaka was remarkable. They met weekly and soon developed a bond of trust and friendship. Kahaska saw in David what he could become some day, and he understood that he had to do his school work and stay out of trouble as a viable avenue for getting there. David and wife, Shelbey, will always remain a part of Kashaka's village. I was pleasantly surprised that my ex-husband, who seldom kept in-touch, endorsed the idea of Kashaka having a mentor and said that he too was mentoring other kids. He was, at that point in time, seriously involved with a lady who had two boys the same age as our kids. He is an educator whose daily interaction with students made him aware of the potential problems that single parents face. It gave us common ground for conversation, and amazingly, over time, our once strained relations became a very cordial and civil friendship.

The Spirit of Racism

Dealing with overt and covert racism was much more of a challenge for me than the cold winter nights. My first real encounter with this demon was at an institution of higher learning in Massachusetts. I was working on a master's degree in education and held a number of short-term campus jobs. I actually floated to departments as the need arose, and this for me was an excellent introduction into understanding the working operations of a campus. Each departmental head had to interview and approve these internship postings. I was eager to serve in the advancement office to learn about grant research and the endowment process. An internship position opened, and I was recommended to fill it. I was called to interview with the departmental head, a Caucasian woman, and felt confident of being chosen. The word around campus was that black people were never chosen to work in the advancement office. When the departmental head invited me into her office to start the interviewing process, she kept repeating my name, Van der Meer, and watching me. She seemed thrown off that I was African American, but I did not want to pre-judge her. We sat down, and her remarks to me were cold and brief. I did not have a fighting chance when she firmly said, "your resume is impressive, and you are in the top five percent; but I have reservations on your ability to perform." This was a staff support position. My mouth dropped open, and I was speechless in disbelief. She said again, "I have reservations on your ability to perform." I asked "Why?" She got openly upset and said, "I do not know; I just have reservations," and she stood up to end the interview. I started to walk to the door, and she said, "This has nothing to do with your qualifications." I could not believe what had just happened in that room, so I went to another departmental head, an African American woman, and related my experience. To my surprise, while she did not approve of her colleague's behavior, she suggested that I take the matter no further because, according to her, my story would create bad press for the institution. I dropped the matter, and about a month later was hired by the same development office.

The director who I had the initial encounter with kept a safe distance from me, never making eye contact. Her two sidekicks, the secretary and her associate, made my time there a living hell. There were many days when the pain of going to work was so overbearing that I cried, fasted, and prayed. The department was revamped in an institutional reorganization. The director was laid off, her secretary was moved to another department, and her associate later lost her job. I graduated and moved on to an appointment at the Massachusetts Board of Regents of Higher Education, and about a year later ran into the associate in my office. She apologized for her behavior and said that the way in which she and her group dealt with me always bothered her. I also had run into the director on the street in Cambridge, Massachusetts. She passed by me as if I did not exist, charging straight ahead. When I returned to that institution as an adjunct professor, the secretary treated me like I was the Queen of Sheba.

Unfortunately my experience of racism was not an isolated one. In my American journey I have also experienced institutional racism that was more covert and embedded in the fabric of the institution and society. While I offer no remedy to its solution, I refuse to sweep it under the carpet when faced with it. My preferred approach is usually direct, using confrontation and communication to highlight and address these issues. Martin Luther King Jr. said, “Injustice anywhere is a threat to justice everywhere.”

Redefining Life's Crossroads

My life was at a crossroads I was balancing family life, giving of myself to my community, serving in the church, developing a personal relationship with Jesus Christ, working two or three jobs (in true Caribbean spirit), and trying to maintain my sanity in an insane environment. Not surprisingly, my body began to feel stretched and burnt out. Many nights I was settling for just four hours of sleep. I had to rethink my priorities. I realized that I was not a superwoman but a woman who must be guided by the Holy Spirit. The vital ingredient that I needed to plot my course was godly wisdom and the guts to simply say no to the demanding request of work. Often, I allowed my compassion and passion for helping others to take precedent over wisdom. I had made myself so accessible to others that I had no privacy. My phone would ring all hours of the day and night. Everybody wanted a favor when, the truth was, I could have done with some favors myself. I was tired of juggling multiple balls, primarily time management, working two jobs, and still having cash flow problems. I felt burned out, yet I continued to extend myself. Everybody wanted something from me, and very few people were inquiring about my well being or that of my kids. Sadly, no one but the doctor seemed to think that I was getting burned out and needed some rest and relaxation. While I have yet to take my doctor's advice on "getting a life," I am now doing better in balancing life. My turning point was when reality hit home.

Reality hit home for me one morning on my way to work, when I almost collapsed on a train packed with rush-hour commuters. I was recovering from a bad cold and disregarded my body's signal to rest. The train had standing room only. I felt like a sick old woman, but apparently I did not look like one, because no one offered to give up their seat, as is often done for the elderly. Every time the trained stopped and moved again, I felt like I was on a roller coaster. My head was spinning, and I started to see people in doubles. Suddenly I could not breathe and was gasping for breath. The train stopped again, and commuters whisked by me as if I were invisible. I pushed forward and stepped off of the train a second before the train door closed. Still gasping for breath, I sat on the bench in the train station and caught my breath. I learned my lesson, to take better care of my body and listen to my body's warning signs.

What amazed me was the selfishness of my supervisor at work when I called in sick that day. She was my friend, and she knew how hard I worked; yet my calling in sick upset her. I would have hoped that this sister, knowing my commitment to work, would have understood and covered my back. Instead, she kept calling my house and hustling me to come back to the office. I started to feel as if she befriended me for professional gain. We were working on the same project and needed to show that we were getting results. I had poured myself into this work and pulled on all of my experiences to jumpstart what was a dying project. Now, I was burning out and felt like I was dying myself. I crawled into bed, took my appointment book, and began to cancel my back-to-back appointments for the next two weeks. I was determined to rest and make some life style changes. My supervisor kept calling to bounce ideas off of me for the project. She actually had no new ideas to offer but welcomed mine, which she incorporated into her report in my absence and took credit for my ideas. Upon my return to work when I learned of this, I confronted her, and she was quite hostile. My ideas were shared as hers; the project was successful, but I got no credit for it. My supervisor very cleverly excluded me from meetings where she continued to present my ideas as hers. This had actually happened to me before in another work related situation. This time, I vowed, must be the last. I became more guarded about sharing my ideas, and, from then on, I documented all of my recommendations and ideas using either email or memorandums. In the long run, I saved myself from office abuse and got credit for my work.

The Webster dictionary defines a *crossroad* as, "A point at which a vital decision must be made."[4] I am sure that I was at that point, having to make the necessary decisions to protect and preserve myself and family. I wanted to leave my children with a legacy of caring for humankind, but I wanted them to employ wisdom in the process and have zero tolerance for abuse of any kind. Self-preservation for me does not mean being selfish, regretting my life's journey, or climbing the corporate ladder just for the satisfaction of seeing everyone else in my rearview mirror. Life means much more to me than that. Self-preservation means setting limits, being able to balance life's demands, knowing when to say no, effectively managing my time, spending more time with my family, and desiring to cultivate a closer walk with God. When I looked at my life and saw the great accolades that my colleagues and the community had bestowed upon me, I was not satisfied. I was honored, but not moved. I knew then that I had to create a more balanced me.

Redefining my crossroads had to come from within. It took life's trials and errors to help me fine tune where I felt I needed to be for functional living. I had to do some self-inventory to determine where I was, had been and needed to go and what avenues would take me there. I treated my life like I was doing an analysis of a corporation. I had to develop a strategic plan to plot out my next steps. I had to be clear on what my goals were and my timelines in achieving those goals and identify with clarity my life mission statement. I determined that my mission is to worship the Lord and be a bridge to connect others to the Lord and his resources. I mapped out a ten-year plan for my life with short-term (three month and one to three-year goals) and long-term goals (seven to ten years). It included these goals:

1. I purchased books on prayer, interviewed old mothers in the church to get advice on praying and other spiritual gems. They talked about holiness as a way of life. I thought, *Lord, I am not ready.* Nevertheless, I set specific times for prayer and fasting, bought and played gospel music during the night, and read my Bible more frequently. The key was in my being consistent, and it proved to be rewarding. It is during this period that I stared to write sermons and preach to myself without having a deep desire to preach to anyone else. I wanted to evangelize but not walk in the role of pastor. In fact, I wrote sermons for five years and preached to myself and my kids for five years before I ever delivered a sermon to a congregation. I was testing the waters and beginning to discover purpose. I was determined to succeed in this effort. Time management was vital. I devised a strategic plan for my life, which included continuing to set aside early mornings for prayer and to be an advocate for my children. This to me constituted good use of my time.

2. At one point in time, I had one child in elementary school, one in middle school, and the other in high school. I attended each of their teachers' conferences and the parent-teacher meetings. I volunteered on school projects and kept a palatable presence in each homeroom teacher's and advisor's face. In this role, I was better able to see the obstacles

that students face at every level of the education system and recognize the importance of parents' involvement in their child's school.

My daughter, Nzinga, was held back from moving on to second grade, for one year. Nzinga's teacher felt that she was a little on the young side and would always end up being the younger kid in the grades ahead, should she be allowed to move up. She feared that Nzinga could be easily influenced by older kids as she progressed through the system if she was allowed to be always the youngest in the class. This teacher had never before taught in a public urban school. She said that, although Nzinga was reading well and academically ready for a second-grade challenge, she was "uncomfortable" with recommending the move. In spite of the protests of Nzinga's godmother (a respected medical doctor and Christian woman), I went along with the decision to hold my daughter back a year. In retrospect, I believed that I made a mistake. Confession is good for the soul.

Nzinga was not adequately being served by repeating a second year of first grade. Although she was ready for second-grade work, her first grade teacher was constantly pulling her back with the bell curve in order to keep pace with the first-grade class. My daughter's enthusiasm for school was waning because she was not challenged, having to repeat first grade. When questions were asked, Nzinga would excitedly raise her hand, knowing the answer, but the teacher would always ignore her. After a while, she sat quietly and seemed disconnected. I was not about to sit back and allow this teacher to break her spirit. The teacher became defensive when I tried to discuss the matter, so I decided to let my presence be felt in the classroom by periodically auditing my child's first-grade class. Nzinga's teacher was visibly uncomfortable by my occasional unannounced class audits and questions pertaining to my child's progress. Around that same time, the school itself was going through another administrative change. As school politics go, the school's principal was unofficially given a vote of no confidence by many staff members. Her unpopularity was rapidly spreading, and her negative interaction with the school's district administrative office was common school gossip. This situation created additional tension and may have affected teachers' performance. However, the principal of the school, who by this time was clearly on her way out, welcomed my interest as a parent advocate. In fact, her desire was to see more parents involved in their children's education. I was not about to compromise the quality of my child's education in this unstable school situation.

I filed for a school district public hearing to have Nzinga moved to a school closer to my home. This was the original school that I had requested for her through the school registration process two years earlier, but, because they had had no openings, she was placed on a waiting list. Somewhere along the line, her name never moved from that waiting list. I was able to acquire the names of students who were accepted into that school and that were waitlisted after my daughter. One, I was told, was never placed on the waiting list but got into the school. The reputation of this elementary public school was very good, and its clientele included children of professionals from Harvard University, Massachusetts Institute of Technology, and the legal and medical circles. Parents at this school were very involved with fundraising and student activities. All I was after was obtaining a good education for my daughter as a fellow taxpayer and parent. My attempts to directly speak with the school personnel about admission were always referred to the parent information center. The parent information center is the unit within the public school system responsible for registration and transfers. This department referred me back to the school, and so the games were on. I felt justified in requesting a school district public hearing to at least be heard. I often wonder how non-English speaking parents or those that speak little English and do not have a college degree are able to navigate this bureaucracy.

Armed with a photo of my daughter mounted in a frame, I headed to the hearing. I also calculated the amount of work time in hours I lost because of having to go to Nzinga's school and the inconvenience those visits caused me. I also felt it was necessary to inform the hearing committee that I was a state employee, a research analyst in the Massachusetts House of Representatives. I wanted to send a message that I was no fool and did not expect to be treated like one. I had a game plan and rehearsed it while driving to the hearing. I was also armed with a few names of kids that were placed ahead of my daughter, just in case all else failed. My goal was not to speak ill of her present school or the first-grade teacher but to get a transfer for my child based on her two years on the school's wait list. I also expected the hearing committee to define for me their waiting list policy, then they would have to help me to understand why the policy was being violated.

When I arrived at the school superintendent's office, I was asked to wait in a hallway where other parents were sitting, awaiting their turns to be heard. I am certain that a number of different school-related problems were on the agenda, but a few were related to school transfers. The scene was tense. Parents were exiting the hearing room visibly upset. One man was just shaking his head and rambling on in another language to a woman at his side. Another woman exited the room in uncontrollable tears. I was the last name to be called for the evening. I entered the room with peace, determined to maintain composure.

There were three people on the hearing

committee. I was asked to sit on what felt like an execution chair. A question was popped at me from the lone male, "So what brings you to see us today." You would have thought he did not know. I replied, "Before I tell you what brought me here today, I want to introduce this committee to my daughter." I opened my large handbag and pulled out the photo of Nzinga, placing it on the desk in front of them. The frame was shining like genuine polished gold. I glanced at the committee, and the man was making eye contact with his colleagues as if to say, what have we got here. Nzinga's beautiful black complexion pierced through the gold photo frame like shiny black silk. Her soft, innocent smile, flashing missing front teeth and thick braids would warm even a phantom's heart. I said to the committee, "I want to introduce you to my daughter, Nzinga. She is a real person. So, when we refer to her in this meeting, I want you to think of her as a person instead of a statistic." The man put his pen down and sat back on his chair, so I reckoned that I had the floor, and I laid out my case. I needed a transfer to a school that was closer to my home, and there was an elementary school just three minutes away, for which Nzinga had been on the waiting list for two years. I indicated that it was my understanding that students who were wait listed after her got into the school. I asked the hearing committee to define the school waiting list policy. The conversation went back and forth but I was not getting anywhere. My goal was to get a transfer. The committee's goal seemed to defend the school department's position that there was no space available at the school I requested. The hearing hit a high note when I asked if the oversight in placing others before my daughter was based on race, class, or socio-economic factors or simply on my lack of knowing the right people in the school system. I was reminded by a woman on the committee that, "this is a public school system," and that these factors would never come into play.

I finally told the committee that if they did not have answers for me that perhaps the board of education might. I also shared that I had the names of kids who were placed ahead of my daughter on the waiting list. Somewhere along the line, the hearing shifted when one of interviewers transitioned the conversation into a friendly chat about political and education issues. My daughter's photo was still center stage. Then, suddenly, the conversation switched back when the woman told a fellow committee member, "We might have just one opening at that school left." He asked if she was sure, and she said she had just remembered. The man said, "Then let's do it." I asked, "How soon?" The woman said she would call the school the following day, and the school would let me know. I asked to have their decision in writing. The man replied that I should not worry about it. In fact, he jokingly said, "You can even pretend that this meeting did not happen." It was already the end of the school year, so Nzinga completed her second year of first grade and was transferred into the new school to start second grade. She still pleasantly talks about her second-grade teachers and may someday tell of her journey through this school in her own memoir.

My advice to parents is to have a visible presence in your child's school. Do not be afraid to ask questions. Recognize that there might be some compromise in the process of balancing and helping the child to settle into a system, but do not take at face value every piece of advice that you receive from the child's teachers. You know your child better than anybody else, and you are your child's best advocate, so do not let a system dictate to you what's best for your child. On the other hand, parents must understand that schools have a mission and are mandated to educate according to a particular curriculum in a specified time frame. Do not be a hindrance for the sake of disagreement. The best method is for school and parent to work together for the common good of the child. Spending time charting my kids' educational course was a priority as I redefined my crossroads.

3. Added to my strategic life plan was careful selection of two or three volunteer activities as opposed to having my hands in everything and burning myself out. For example, I continued to work at the food

pantry and serve on the board of trustees at a charter school in Cambridge. My prior eight years as a board member at a seminary had left me with a wealth of experience and pleasant memories of service.

4. Next, I identified my children's academic interests and exposed them to the stimulation necessary to keep them motivated. For example, I enrolled my then seven-year-old daughter in a summer science camp that taught her how to build and launch rockets, and we frequently visited the science museum in Boston. Now, at seventeen, she still loves natural science. Her goal is to become a biochemist.

5. I had a goal to write a curriculum unit and would have been satisfied even if I was never given the opportunity to teach from my curriculum unit. I first had to learn how to write curriculum units. I took a graduate-level course with Professor Lynne Sussman. Lynne was a graduate of Harvard University and a very thorough woman. In her class, once I understood the concept and format of writing curriculum units, I began to connect threads and see creative ways of introducing a subject matter. Lynne took me under her wing during my time in her class, and I did very well in that course.

   Years later, I wrote a curriculum unit and taught it to seventh and eighth graders in two Catholic schools in Cambridge, Massachusetts. I later wrote another one entitled "Community Change and Development (from a Socio-Economic and Political Perspective)" and was employed to teach it to McNair Scholars at a Massachusetts state college summer institute. This accomplished yet another goal and brought me a sense of self-gratification. Next!

6. I started a daily exercise plan of jogging and walking with the aim of keeping fit.

7. Next was to stop eating fast food and start eating healthier foods.

8. Another goal was to publish my memoirs.

I have conquered my first ten-year goal plan and am currently working on my second ten-year plan, in which I am ahead of the timelines that I had set for myself. Hooray! After all of this hard work, a close friend asked me if I had room for a husband in my life. Well, of course I do, but I was not consumed by the thought, neither was it high on my list of priorities. My God knows how to give good gifts and blesses us with the desire of our hearts.

Redefining my life did not always work according to my charted plan. I am not a mechanical being. There were times when I did not know what was going on. At these times, I had to sit tight and ride out the storms in prayer, not knowing the outcome. I simply trusted God to take me through, and I worked with the outcomes. In the process, I developed increasing faith and positioned myself for God's use.

In Receipt of the Mandate

Count Down

Positioning oneself for God's use means different things to different people. For me, it meant obeying the statutes of God and developing a closer walk with God. I allowed my work and actions to speak as a testimony to my Christian living. I practiced humility, kindness, and gentleness but still lacked patience. I told others about Jesus, helped college-bound youths prepare for college, and supported my pastor's vision for the church. I was quite satisfied in these roles. Positioning, for me, never meant serving in the role of pastor. I was comfortable in a supporting role, but God had a different plan for my life.

My pastor kept encouraging me to become more active as a lay minister by teaching Bible study every Wednesday evening. After a year or so of in-house training, I started to teach the Wednesday adult Bible study class. This was a challenge that forced me to spend more time studying the Bible and to develop a greater dependence on the Holy Spirit. I was ready to answer the call of God on my life. Occasionally, I was asked to preach. I always remember being scared stiff. I was doing all the right things but I realized that I had lost my joy. My prayer was for joy to return. It did and I promised never to let the stresses of life steal my joy again. Every year for seven years, I set aside a time close to the end of the year to specifically seek the Lord for a personal word of encouragement and direction for the New Year.

Year # 1

Jeremiah 1:9, "Then the Lord put forth his hand and touched my mouth. And the Lord said unto me, 'Behold, I have put my words in thy mouth'" (KJV).

I knew that the coming year would be a time when I would speak out boldly about the things of God with greater confidence and greater comfort in yielding to the leading of the Holy Spirit. Prior to this, I was sometimes very timid when asked to pray in certain situations, such as a community event.

Year # 2

Isaiah 41:6, "…be of good courage" (KJV).

That year, the more that I prayed, the more everything went wrong in my life. Things were just not falling into place. Every area of my life felt under great attack as I dealt with one situation after another. When I tried to tell a friend my woes, she was thrilled, telling me, "Hold on to God because you are at a great point for God to work in your life. The battle has already been won." Well, if this was winning, I shuddered to experience losing. I felt that my friend needed to get her head checked, but I took her advice anyway and kept on praying and pressing forward.

Year #3

Isaiah 50:4, "The Lord had given me the tongue of the learned, that I should know how to speak a word in season to him that is weary: he wakeneth morning by morning, he wakeneth mine ear to hear as the learned" (KJV).

I continued to write sermons. I was counseling and praying for others with such frequency that my home telephone was primarily used as a prayer line. This launched my telephone ministry, and I started to teach Bible study via telephone to the sick and elderly and to friends in other countries and states. Thank God for technology.

Year # 4

Isaiah 6:8, "Also, I heard the voice of the Lord' saying, whom shall I send, and who will go for us? Then said I, Here am I; send me" (KJV).

By this time, I had submitted to cleansing,

purification, and sanctification through periods of fasting, prayer, reading the bible, attending ministerial trainings, and repenting. I saw my faults. For example, there was a time when my kids were taking the place of God because my life revolved around them to an extent that I did not make adequate time to spend in the word of God. Now, I am better able to balance both.

Year #5

Romans 1:17, " For therein is the righteousness of God revealed from faith to faith: as it is written, The just shall live by faith" (KJV).

Daily I read and recited the Scriptures on faith because at times, when faced with challenges, I doubted myself. Once I began to put my trust more in the Lord and recognize that I was being taken through a process in life, I was able to increase my faith.

Year #6

Proverbs 3: 5–6, "Trust in the Lord with all thine heart; and lean not unto thine own understanding. In all thy ways acknowledge him, and he shall direct thy paths" (KJV).

My challenges were getting greater, and I was pulling strength from the Word of God. Some days all I had to stand on was my trust in the Lord.

Some days, I grew so weak from battle that I could only whisper, "I am trusting in you, Lord. For your Word says, the just must live by faith." I knew that God was with me. I felt God's grace and the comforting reassuring touch of the Holy Spirit in spite of family illnesses and deaths.

Year #7

Galatians 5:25, "If we live in the spirit, let us also walk in the Spirit" (KJV).

I needed to better understand the position of living in the Spirit and the posture of walking in the Spirit. I listened to a sermon from Pastor Benny Hinn on this subject that brought such clarity to my understanding that my next step was to live it.

The Prophecy

I moved from Cambridge to Quincy, Massachusetts, joined another church, and years later was ordained as a pastor. The bishop in the ordination service said the Lord told him I was to launch out and spread the Gospel. He told me I would minister to heads of government and leaders and that the Lord would use me to bring backsliders back to him and to win many souls. I had heard the same words spoken over my life from three other pastors in separate circumstances years earlier. Doors had since opened for me to spread the Gospel of Jesus Christ to members of parliament, the judiciary system, and the Diplomatic Corp in the Caribbean, including a representative of the United Nations as well as the Organization of American States. The bishop looked me straight in the eye at my ordination service and said, "Pray that the Lord will give you a womb to build that church in Florida." I had lingered in God's permissive will for too long and was now ready to go all the way for the Lord, without quite having a working definition of going all the way.

I always felt that I needed to be doing something else but could never quite put my finger on what that something else was. Once I gained a better clarity of the Word of the Lord, it was easier for me to desire whatever God's prefect will was for my life. I voluntarily surrendered to God and relinquished my will for his, laboring in the house of God and positioning myself to serve and learn. Periodically, I continued to write my prayer thoughts in a book. Habakkuk 2:2-4, reads:

> And the Lord answered me, and said, Write the vision, and make it plain upon tables, that he may run that readeth it. For the vision is yet for an appointed time, but at the end it shall speak, and not lie: though it tarry, wait for it; because it will surely come, it will not tarry. Behold, his soul which is lifted up is not upright in him: but the just shall live by his faith.
>
> Habakkuk 2:2–4 (KJV)

The Vision

The vision to plant a church was a clear assignment and calling on my life that had the affirmation, sanction, and blessing of my church and bishop. I was continuously assured by my peers in ministry that it was God's work and the Lord Jesus would protect and provide for me. I must admit, while those were very comforting words, my real comfort level came when there was some tangible pledge to support this ministry while I relocated to Florida to start Living Water Christian Fellowship and seek additional secular employment. The financial pledges and moral support from churches and individuals actually made my transition more manageable. I was humbled by the task that God had entrusted to me. As a sign of my total commitment, I invested my time and financial resources to make it work. We had two families on the ground in Florida that were working with me at that end and three families in Massachusetts who were planning to relocate to help build Living Water.

For a time, mine was the only family (my thirteen-year-old daughter, Nzinga, and I) that relocated, while the other three families were working on joining us at a later date. Nzinga had a difficult time in the first year because she missed her friends, but she wanted to support her mom. While she never complained, we had very open discussions on the matter. She soon adjusted to life in Boca Raton, Florida and made new friends, still remaining connected to those she left behind in Quincy and Cambridge, Massachusetts.

In the mean time, I was pregnant with this project and making every preparation for a healthy church planting in Florida. Accountability had to be a primary factor in this start-up ministry, and an open channel of communication was a necessity. We put together a vibrant board and a skilled advisory council, including former church planters. Our first board meeting was a great milestone, and it generated much passion for the vision. The board committed to daily prayer on early morning conference calls for the first and second year of ministry and ongoing regular prayers for the ministry thereafter. At least one board member still calls me daily to pray.

Prayer has made a tremendous difference in my efforts to establish a church. It has kept me more connected and in tune with God. I have created a bond with the board members that help us to be free to criticize and disagree on issues and be frank and honest with each other. I have trusted the board's judgment and have learned not to make decisions without wise counsel. The congregation, Advisory Council, and board kept me accountable to the tenets of our faith, the overall functioning of the church, and to each other.

The mission of Living Water Christian Fellowship International is to turn the heart of man to Christ and create end-time thinkers for an end-time harvest. How is this to be accomplished? By reaching into ourselves and out to others through the following:

- Developing the fruit of the spirit
- Christian discipleship

- Not forsaking the cry of the poor
- Pursuing personal spiritual growth
- Reaching local and international students.

1. *Development of the fruit of the spirit*

   "But the fruit of the spirit is love, joy, peace, longsuffering, gentleness, goodness, faith, meekness, temperance: against this there is no law" (Galatians 5: 22–23, KJV).

   This is a lifetime aspiration that I continue to strive to develop as a point of duty. I encourage others to do the same. I hold the opinion that worship cannot be effectively achieved without the presence of the fruit of the spirit in operation within my life, and this is necessary for end-time survival.

2. *Christian discipleship*

   The Bible charges us to spread the Gospel of Jesus Christ Mark 16:15, "And he said unto them, Go ye into all the world, and preach the gospel to every creature" (KJV).

   At Living Water Christian Fellowship, we plant seeds in the hope of cultivating disciples for Christ. Street ministry is a part of our on-going efforts to reach others

3. *Do not forsake the cry of the poor.*

   Proverbs 19:17 states, "He that hath pity upon the poor lendeth unto the Lord; and that which he hath given will he pay him again" (KJV). How awesome to have an opportunity to lend to God. My goal at Living Water is to help care for the poor and to teach others by example. As a young church we have come to the aid of hurricane victims in New Orleans and the Caribbean and have reached out to single parents in our community. A few people can indeed make a difference. I intend to please God.

4. *Nourishment of personal spiritual growth*

Nourishment of personal spiritual growth is another mandate for me individually and for all of us as a church community. There were periods in my life when I neglected self (physically and spiritually), but I have since corrected that by eating healthier foods, exercising regularly, reading the Bible for personal Bible study, praying, and fasting with more frequency and consistency. I am practicing what I preach—a healthy lifestyle. It is because of this level of maturity that I accomplished a balance in life and growth in Christ that brings personal satisfaction. In this frame of mind, it is truly easier for me to minister to others, allowing my life to be an example.

5. *Reaching local and international students.*

Years before I became a pastor, while attending graduate school Christian fellowship meetings, the Holy Spirit said to me, "...in preparation for the end-time harvest, I will again move on the campuses. A revival will burst out on college campuses across America and the face of education will be changed because I will show myself as God. Even professors who are atheists and philosophers will join the campus revival movement." I was amazed and shared these thoughts with my advisor, who was a well-respected ordained minister and professor. His response was cold and defensive, as if he felt he needed to defend the current academic climate that denied Christianity in favor of science and philosophy. His reaction also could have been a direct result of his religious orientation. Many denominations do not belief in prophecy, although I do not see myself as a prophet. Our conversation went no further, but I could not help but thinking that the oldest academic institution in America was founded on the principles of Christianity and so was our country. It was my hope and desire to be, some day, an integral part of campus ministry to spread the Gospel to national and international students.

Two years after we started Living Water Christian Fellowship, I was asked by a group of university students to teach a Bible study twice a week on campus. These sessions soon turned into church services with vibrant praise and worship and teaching sermons. I had already been conducting prayer and Bible study with another university group outside of campus, hosted at a student's home. I was humbled to be a part of these national and international students' village. Each week our sessions grew, one and two at a time. There was such trust and bonding that I often felt like the house mother. I even gave up a few Saturdays and weekday evenings to attend different functions that my Bible study students invited me to, in support of their extracurricular campus activities, for example, Model United Nations.

At Living Water I had a lot on my plate, but I recognized that I had to trust in the Lord and ensure that I did not develop into a one-man show. This was kingdom building, and I simply was an end-time kingdom servant. The Lord sent me to Palm Beach county. I mapped out two areas to start ministries in: Boca Raton and Riviera Beach. Our targeted audience was youth and the un-churched population with an emphasis on backsliders and newcomers as we spread the Gospel of Jesus Christ. I was operating in my "calling" and felt like I was walking in God's perfect will for my life.

In my first one hundred days of ministry in Florida I:

1. Created another arm of the ministry called the Prayer Connection Network.

   This network was comprised of prayer intercessors locally, nationally, and international to specifically pray for my family, the ministry and me. I later filtered other prayer requests through this group.

2. Implemented a street ministry.

   I wanted to get a feel for my targeted areas in a way that no demographic data could truly describe. Street ministry was hard. Maybe it was my approach. I walked up and greeted people in a political campaign style. As I walked the lonely streets in my neighborhood, it suddenly dawned on me that in Boca Raton, people drove everywhere. It was not like Boston where you would see people hustling down the street to catch the next train or bus. I had taken my big city life experience for granted, and now I was missing it, stuck in Boca unable to walk to my favorite ice-cream store, Toscanini's, in Harvard Square. I decided that street ministry might be a bad idea after all so I hit my neighborhood gym in Boca Raton to do gym ministry. The gym was filled with people, but it seemed more remote than the street because no one had the time or desire to talk. Their goals were clear: get in, get pumped, and get out. Rejected, I was determined to reach people if only I could find them. I changed my timing and hit the streets again. It worked. This was to be my pilot project before I employed a team to go with me. I was also being informally educated about my surroundings. For example, I had to start jogging to blend into the culture. I hate to jog. On my first morning jog, I came home panting like a thirsty dog.

   I was beginning to feel the beat of Florida. Every day I saw the same people on my exercise route, and, before long, friendly exchanges developed, which open a door for evangelizing. This turned out to be a very rewarding experience because through this ministry, one by one, we added to Living Water, and I built new acquaintances; for example my friend, Peggy, whom I met during my street ministry. She was a member of a church in the area but committed to praying for me. Every morning as she walked in front of my condominium, she stopped and prayed for me. Another woman called out to me and shared that she had observed me praying as I walked and this convicted her to start praying again. The work had begun. One Sunday morning, I looked at the congregation and everyone present was as a result of street ministry. Amen.

3. Started a Sunday service in my home.

A few hours before my first service, I felt overwhelmed as I went into prayer. The Holy Spirit spoke the following, "Be bold my precious flower, do not be intimidated, but speak my Word. I have called you for this season. Listen to my voice, and my eyes will guide you." I was encouraged.

We held services in my living room for about three weeks before securing a meeting space at an area school cafeteria for Sunday worship. At this opening, twenty-one people attended, including my mother and aunt, who traveled from another country for the opening and another old aunt who lived in an elderly facility in the neighboring Coral

Spring City. They attended and pronounced their blessings upon me and the ministry as their stamp of approval.

4. Made courtesy calls to church, city and community leaders.

I contacted other pastors and community leaders in my area, requesting a courteous visit to introduce myself and ministry. This proved to be quite a challenging exercise. I needed a little encouragement, so I contacted a friend and pastor who lived in another state. His comments added to my pain. He said that I had "too much passion for ministry." He cautioned me based on his own experience. He said, "While there is passion in every vision, one has to wake up to something called reality." The "reality" he identified was having a secure financial base to survive in Florida. He predicted that when reality hit, I would drop the passion and "move on." He explained the bills have to be paid and food must be on the table, but that jobs are hard to find in South Florida. All true. He spoke from his personal experience and told me that to survive I had to "leave the vision behind." He relocated from Florida to New Jersey. I could tell by the tone of his voice that his life was miserably unfulfilled. I did not let his negativity get to me because I believed I must be passionate about my vision and communicate it to others for implementation or risk losing it. Passion and vision

> cannot be separated. It is the key to winning. As my friend spoke to me, I felt sorry for him. I wanted to tell him that my Lord is a God of passion and reality, but I kept my peace. I learned a valuable lesson to not share my vision with just anyone and to keep my eyes on Jesus. I had developed a mindset that if the ministry went under I would still be praising the Lord. I proceeded to build the ministry fearlessly with great passion and trust in God.

My telephone calls to pastors and community leaders to request a courtesy call meeting were met with some outright rejections. Some never returned my calls but a few were quite cordial. A rabbi who declined to meet with me offered his advice for survival in ministry. He suggested that I meet with funeral home owners in my area and concentrate on burying the dead as a steady source of income. No kidding.

An Episcopal priest looked me up and down and, smiling, he said, "I admire you." One city official said that he accepted my meeting because he was curious to see who could be so bold to demand to meet the head when his office suggested that I met with someone lower down the ranks. He was cute, too. At another meeting, a priest suggested that I pack up and leave town because, according to him, the people of Boca Raton's spiritual needs were already adequately being met. Oh really! My line remained the same at each courtesy call meeting. I introduced myself, gave a little background data, and talked about Living Water to let them know that we existed and could co-exist in ministry as a moral support base for each other.

I could tell a few of these guys were not ready for a woman in ministry or a vocal one. I recognized that I was politely being whisked through the old boys' network and getting nowhere. Having worked at the state level in Massachusetts, I readily understood the old boys' network games. These guys in Boca were pretending to "let me in" by giving me referrals to other network churches and wasting my time with "pass the buck" syndrome. Everybody wanted to get me out of their faces but hoped for the next guy to do the job. The key that kept me going was that I did not need the Boca Raton religious community to define for me my mandate in Christ. As a result, my goal was not to look for their approval or acceptance.

One lead that I followed up on was a female rabbi. We immediately connected. She shared the initial rejection and difficulty that she experienced at the hand of her male counterparts. She said that across religious and denomination lines there was a general lack of welcome for women in ministry in South Florida. I might add that this is not characteristic of just south Florida. This female rabbi told me that she ignored those who ignored her and weathered the storm of rejection. After eleven years in ministry, she now gets a better reception from peers and has earned respect in the community. She said that she was one of only approximately five hundred female rabbis in the world and had fought to earn respect and maintain her office. We encouraged each other, and I was energized as I kept on course.

Next, I attended a clergy luncheon hosted by a local hospital. I wore a clergy collar and was not the only person dressed in clergy attire, but I was the only female clergy representative. An old Baptist minister turned to me and said, "I know that you are a pastor, but why are you wearing a collar?" Interestingly enough, he did not ask any of the men that question. It took Christ in me to keep from telling him, "It's a new style!" He said, "Non-denominational churches do not wear collars." I held my peace for fear of having to repent should I have answered him.

The funniest meeting that I had was with a Catholic priest, the same one that earlier suggested that I pack up and leave. He said I should really consider taking my ministry elsewhere to be able to, "catch a few fish that looked like me." He discussed his love for all people and shared that his church was multicultural and filled with parishioners who were not about to change their minds from Catholicism. Okay, time to move on. I met with another pastor about the possibility of sharing rental space at his church. He looked at me with a poker face and said, "Never. When you start to preach, I will lose my people to you full-Gospel folks." I was amused.

My encounters continued when an area business woman and lay minister connected me to her pastor whom she said hosted several meetings with neighborhood pastors. This pastor was collaborating to start prayer walks in Boca Raton. My friend said that the group had been meeting monthly for coffee round table discussions to develop strategies for implementing street ministry and prayer walks in Boca Raton. Our church, Living Water, was now in its second year of street ministry and prayer walks. This woman was confident that I would be an excellent addition to this group, particularly since Living Water accomplished much in this geographic area. She herself had come to know me through our prayer walk and street ministry efforts. Some mornings, I would stop at her business place and pray for her, her employees, and the community. I was motivated to reach out to this pastor, and as a church, we were open to collaboration.

I telephoned this pastor, who appeared to be offended at the fact that a new church was walking the streets of Boca Raton in prayer for the community. He kept on asking "You are a new church and doing this?" He said that his church was planning to be the front runner in this area as the "first in Boca." I thought maybe if his coffee-drinking group had reached out to a few women, they could have gotten the job done two years ago. Nevertheless, I expressed my desire to attend one of their monthly meetings in anticipation of him inviting me. He bypassed that bait, so I was more direct in suggesting that our church join with their group to collaborate planning these community prayer walks. He quickly agreed and faithfully promised to call me back. He never did, nor did he return my subsequent calls. It is sad. I was looking forward to collaborating, because interceding in prayer for a city takes spiritual leaders with an anointing to deal with territorial spirits. This would have been an opportunity to work together for kingdom purpose.

Gatekeeper

I did not know what to think about the reception that I was getting from spiritual leaders in Boca Raton. Are these gatekeepers, and is it all about protecting territory or defending the profession? I continued to reach out, meeting with another faith leader. One of them had a simple solution for gaining visibility and acceptance in Boca Raton. He told me I must try to position Living Water to emulate the traditional churches that are located on Yamato Road and start by renting space from one of these churches to set up Sunday shop. Yamato Road is a street in Boca Raton where beautiful, historically designed church buildings line the street in architectural splendor. I later had the opportunity to pray for a pastor from one of these churches. A hurricane named Wilma hit Boca Raton, damaging many churches. The pastor said to me, "God must be speaking to the churches in Florida. We need to focus more on doing God's work." I could not agree more. He asked me to continue to pray for him.

I continued making my rounds among the faith-based community in Boca Raton. One lay minister suggested that I visit a popular evangelical church in the area to be able to "pattern from it" to "gain acceptance." The last thing that I was looking for was to run a ministry by a formula. A female pastor, believing that she was giving me the inside scoop for cracking into the Boca religious sects, strongly suggested that I "dress like the women in ministry in South Florida." I certainly was not prepared to compromise my identity to imitate the style of someone else. I am who I am, black and natural in the splendor of beauty, and I am proud of it. These ministerial well-wishers were getting more ridiculous by the minute, and I was disgusted by their remarks. I was convinced that Living Water must continue to seek and be guided by directives from the Lord. And I, as a pastor and chief servant, am accountable to the Lord, my bishop, my board, and my congregation.

I had the opportunity to meet a few key Boca Raton city officials and to talk about Living Water. The mayor, a Jewish man with New England roots, was more cordial to me than any of the clergy. With sound political savvy, he accepted an invitation to speak at a Living Water gospel concert. Next, I paid a courtesy call to the Boca Raton Chief of Police and shared goals of the ministry. I was in the process of planning Living Water's first annual youth conference and wanted to involve the city, police, health, and school departments as speakers and role models. The reception was good. Ministry for me is much more than a Sunday morning sermon. I want to contribute to help chart a positive direction for young people. My meeting with Chief Scott was energizing and encouraging because he, too, cared about the plight of young people within and beyond the borders of Boca Raton. He shared my passion.

While I was passionate about the work of the Lord and was not easily discouraged, I was disgusted by the lack of cooperation and civility among clergy in my area. Many of them were outright arrogant and sexist. One pastor helped me to understand the culture. He said that churches pop up in south Florida with such frequency and with "rebel" leadership that pastors are very cautious to open up to someone new unless a track record has been established. I got it. I understood that their comments were not a personal attack on me as an individual per se but that the gatekeepers were protecting their turf. Some of them were dealing with their church's denominational concept of who should or should not be in ministry. The fact that I am a black female divorced single parent posed a challenged for some of these guys more than the ministry being new. I took the punches but continued to implement the vision that God had given me while I waited for second rounds with these gatekeepers.

After a couple years of being in the area, a few gatekeepers opened up but kept a safe distance. However, I was able to form some close associations with about nine other local churches and developed a wonderful working relationship with their pastors. I continued to solicit advice in ministry and across the board, which I will share in the next chapter. I was now in my fourth year in ministry in South Florida. One summer we temporarily lost our church meeting space because the building had to undergo repairs. A Lutheran pastor whom I had met a year or so before graciously came to my rescue. He provided us with free meeting space on Sundays and Wednesdays and allowed us the aid of his secretary all summer long. The secretary worked cheerfully and tirelessly at completing

Living Water Youth Summit program book. May God bless them.

Disappointment in Ministry

Longevity in ministry for me was contingent upon being able to sustain a disciplined prayer life and operate in the wisdom of God, with faith as my weapon of defense. Financial support was also of vital importance to sustaining a ministry. My disappointments came when my mentor and a senior person in ministry whom I trusted and respected made a financial pledge for ongoing support to the ministry and did not honor it. A couple times he assured me that the "check was in the mail," but his empty promises kept coming. It really was more about the trust factor than the financial support. I felt hurt and even questioned my judgment of characters.

A young ministry depends on and utilizes every penny that comes in just for operational cost. In Luke 14: 28 there is a biblical principle of adding up the cost, which I would imagine includes preparing a projected budget in a dollar figure, although one could never calculate the true cost of ministry. It is immeasurable. We did some prior planning and budgetary projections, but faith was also factored in to accomplish our purpose. It was vital for me to remember that it was God's church, not mine. Matthew 16:18, "And I say also unto thee, That thou art Peter, and upon this rock I will build my church: and the gates of hell shall not prevail against it" (KJV). Now I look to God to support the ministry through man. When we come up short in the church budget, I look to the Lord and not the mail box, awaiting empty promises.

Bid Them Come

It is no secret that breaking new ground is a difficult task. I am always comforted by the fact that I was called to this ministry. Nevertheless, I have had some dark days when all my efforts seemed in vain, but I recognized that it is in these times that I need to keep praying and moving according to the plan. I periodically do an inventory to determine and reflect on what is working and what's not in the ministry.

I had been doing street ministry at least four times a week, and, overall, things were looking up for this church-plant. Our first one hundred days in ministry went off without a hitch, but now, on a personal level, I was feeling burnt out and isolated. I felt that I needed a partner in ministry. It was during this time that I thought about remarrying for companionship in ministry. I have been celibate for many years. The good news was that for the first time in my life I felt complete within my being, in which my mind, body, and soul were totally in sync. I am extremely comfortable with self, and this is priceless, a good sign that I am ready for that level of commitment. In the meantime, I draw strength from my daily early morning prayer group. Often after our prayer sessions, I feel a refreshing of the spirit, ready to evangelize.

Water with the Blood

I was eager to see more growth at Living Water, but it was scriptural for me to bring my anxiety under subjection, while also recognizing that success of a ministry should not be merely measured by numbers. I employed the principle of David Yonggi Cho, author of *Successful Home Cell Groups,* to pray specifically for each individual church goal that I had, subject to the will of God. The word of the Lord came to me while interceding for the ministry, and I heard, "Water the seed that you have planted with my blood." It revolutionized my prayer for Living Water. In prayer, I took that seed that was planted called Living Water Christian Fellowship, and I saturated it with the blood of Jesus. I visualized the roots of a young plant growing into a full-grown tree.

It was working. Souls were being won for Jesus under this ministry. In fact, at our second service, a teenaged Jewish girl gave her heart to Christ, and her mother recommitted hers. Since then, many souls have come to Christ under Living Water Ministry. Also, I have been humbled to be able to lay hands on the tummies of pregnant women. I have prayed for approximately one hundred fifty unborn babies. I meet pregnant woman on the street, at church, at malls, in the doctor's office, and even in line at the supermarket checkout counter. This, for a season, was a busy ministry. However, street and campus ministries still remain my strongest source for evangelizing.

From the Horse's Mouth

Labor Pains

The struggles in ministry and, in particular, the initial stages of church planting were intense and sacrificial. There seemed to always be limited resources to go around, but I never was in lack. While sometimes, help came not as quickly as I would have liked, God's timing is always the right time. What was most frustrating to me in my early days as a church planter was the attitude of a couple friends and family members who did not have a clue about ministry and were not even saved but presented themselves to me as the authority on church affairs and expected me to act upon their unsolicited advice. One man even objected to renting space for the church to meet in, suggesting that we find a basement somewhere in Florida instead. The only problem was Florida houses do not traditionally have basements. Another suggested that praise and worship time should be kept to "no more than fifteen minutes." This woman was not even a member.

This type of unsolicited advice was so frequent that I had to carefully screen my telephone calls.

A word that I received deep in my spirit was that I should not let spiritual poachers frighten me, those takers who just stopped by to get my ideas for their own use. The Lord said, "It is my church, do not keep it strapped to your bosom." This would stifle the work and render both me and the ministry ineffective, so I am always open to sharing ideas with other ministers and looking for collaboration in ministry. However, I use wisdom and know when to be silent, even when there is an opportunity to speak.

On a personal level, finding a secular job in Florida was like searching for a needle in a haystack. This was a constant source of discouragement to me. Many days, I contemplated moving on, but my commitment and passion for the ministry kept me going. There were some days when I felt like crumbling under the burden. God chastised me as I travailed in fasting and praying, "Never let the work that you do for me be a burden, for then I will not accept it as your sacrifice." I felt like the prophet Isaiah, "Woe is me." I have since learned to release my burdens to Jesus. My personal goal is to seek the joy of the Lord because the joy of the Lord is my strength.

Bishop Hessie Lee Harris spoke these words to me when I was leaving Boston for Florida, and it became a tune in my ear and a source of strength. He said, "It is not important for others to praise you after you give a sermon because the same persons who praise you will cut you down when you speak the truth." He cautioned me not to gauge my performance on affirmations from the congregation but to base my ministry on, "the integrity of preaching the gospel." With such sound advice, I decided to go fishing in search of more.

Advice from the Horse's Mouth

Good advice is always valuable, but there is a premium placed on advice that comes from a person who speaks from personal experiences. I interviewed the real experts to help me frame some lessons and was able to draw strength from these frontline church pioneers. I consider myself privileged to have had this opportunity. As I share these words of wisdom with you, it is my hope that you, too, can glean strength from them. Each is unique because it is someone else's account viewed through their experiences. Collectively, this sound advice can be used as a standard for how to succeed in ministry.

I asked each person the same question, "From your experience, what advice do you have for me in ministry?" Here is what I got.

Advice #1: From Mother Ward (now deceased), the wife of a pastor

"Let your ministry be rooted in prayer; read the Bible and follow God."

Advice #2: From a rabbi

"Think about generating an income to help sustain you while in ministry and recognize the importance of developing solid relationships within the area of ministry."

Advice # 3: From a Boca Raton pastor

"This [Boca Raton] is a different area. It has its own personality. Be aware of your image. As you add folks, know their needs and make your facility and program appropriate."

Advice # 4: From a Catholic priest

"Be patient, be regional, and know your area of ministry."

Advice # 5: From, Dr. Randy MacFarland, Vice President of Denver Seminary

"Read the book of Acts, chapter 18 verses 9–10: "' Then spake the Lord to Paul in the night by a vision, Be not afraid, but speak, and hold not thy peace. For I am with thee, and no man shall set on thee to hurt thee: for I have much people in this city'" (KJV).

Advice # 6: From Rev. Dr. Paul Bothwell

"Learn about fundraising and the different approaches to it. Build on your relationships, knowledge and resources. Ask yourself what you have that benefits others that would make them willing to collaborate with you. "It is a process called 'system thinking'" he said, "and you must employ it." He suggested that I read a book, *The Fifth Discipline* by Peter Senge.

Advice # 7: From Pastor Herman Bryant, a trusted friend and fellow church planter

"Walk in faith and trust God. Resist the devil; know yourself and your purpose and do not be afraid to walk through the doors of favor that God will open for you."

Advice # 8: From Pastor James Archer, founder of the Adventist Congregational Church, Cambridge, Massachusetts.

"Walk in faith and be guided by the Holy Spirit. In any situation, always ask yourself, what would Jesus have done? Always remember that God is with you."

Advice # 9: From Apostle Allen

"Just obey God."

Advice # 10: From Pastor Jennifer

"Know your strengths and weaknesses; do not be shy to ask others for help; welcome, without bias, anyone who comes to your Church; and go wherever the Lord leads you."

Advice #11: From a female rabbi

"Know who you are and do not be intimidated.

Always remember that you have just as much right to be a worker of God as any male counterpart."

Advice # 12: From Bishop Hessie Lee Harris

"Stay focused, trust God, preach the gospel, and share the church's need with the congregation. In church planting, you must experience transition before transformation, after which, comes suffering. As shepherds, we must understand suffering. All ministries must go through the blood and the fire. It is only then that we would be able to lead a flock and buffer the kinds of things that come up against us in ministry."

Advice # 13: From my aunt Judy Davies

"I admire your boldness. Follow the leading of God and make sure that you hear from God and not what people think is best for your ministry. Amen!"

Advice # 14: From an area pastor, Palm Beach County, Florida

"Be faithful to your calling, seek first the kingdom of God, and learn to love all people."

Advice # 15: From another area pastor, West Palm Beach, Florida

"Be faithful in the little things, and God will make you responsible for much; and always think Scripture."

Advice # 16: From a friend, Joseph Jeffers

"Rely on the Lord for all of your needs in ministry."

Advice # 17: From Pastor Novlett Rhoden-Robinson

"Do not be dismayed because the Lord will never leave nor forsake you."

Advice #18: From Bishop Glen Prospere, Boston, Massachusetts

"Do not let your personal emotions get in the way of ministry because you will get hurt. When disappointments and trials in ministry come, you have to deal with it on two levels, from the stand point of ministry and as an individual. It is the way in which a situation is handled that earns the pastor respect by the people."

Advice #19: From Sister Gemma Maharaj, a dear friend and first lady Westend Christian Fellowship in Trinidad, West Indies

"In ministry you must take authority and declare the Word of God. Keeping a positive attitude as well as developing good eating habits is important to physical and spiritual well being. Ask a few people to commit to interceding for the pastor and family and always remember that the battle is not yours, it is the Lord's. Do not get into the system of putting a price tag on the gospel by asking for money for everything, the people can't give what they do not have."

Advise # 20: From Rev. Dr. T. Allen Bethel, Portland, Oregon

"Keep your vision in a place where you can see it and remind yourself of it. Share the vision of the church with others as they come. Do not waste time on those who are not interested in the vision. Time is important and in ministry you have to prioritize and do not let people waste your time at the ministry's expense.

Congregation building is a process in which you would be able to distinguish primarily two groups of people as you build relationships. The individuals that are less productive, often they seek to change the vision. One set requires a lot of your time, for out of this group are your leaders. The process is evolving as new people come and attach themselves; tension could sometime arise between new and old. Keep in mind that the vision is what God gave you. The vision is not up for debate. The vision is the vision. Set standards of accountability and put them on the table early."

Advice # 21: From Sister Olive Knight, my dear friend

"Stay in his will."

Advice # 22: From Aunt Marjorie King

"Many churches start small, but you must be

confident in the Lord, be persistent and patient; and God will keep his work."

Advice # 23: From Rev. Dr. Aimraj Maharaj, Pastor Westend Christian Fellowship, Trinidad, West Indies

"Know your calling and do not compare or compete with anyone else. As God opens doors and you walk through them, the whole picture for your ministry purpose begins to unfold. Not every day will be sunny because if every day was sunny, the world would be a desert. We need the sun and the rain. When both are combined, you will receive the desired effect."

Advice # 24: From Pastor Dianne Van der Meer

I add my own voice to this collection of advice for others as well as for myself.

Stand firm without compromising the gospel. Work with the wheat and the tares of your ministry, but pray for the spirit of discernment to know the difference.

Advice # 25: From Mummy Yvonne

My mother, friend, and prayer intercessor put the icing on the cake of advice with her deep words of motherly wisdom: "Trust God, make time for yourself, and take an afternoon nap every day. I am touched by God's hand upon your life, and your love for Jesus. I admire that in faith, you fight for what you want. Go forward and do what God

> called you to do." That's a caring mom. Her words blessed my soul.

I am grateful for all the words of encouragement and advice. I know that no textbook or seminary course could have been more conclusive. When challenges present themselves in ministry, and they have, I revisit these words of wisdom and find comfort. I am truly humbled by those that have taken the time to share from their own journey to enrich my walk with God. It is my desire to share this information with others in ministry and, in particular, potential church planters.

Conclusion

I might have wandered through life's journey, but I was never aimless. I always had purpose as my driving force, even when my purpose was not well defined. Writing this book helped me to reflect on and revisit areas in my life that I would have preferred to forget. But it also helped me to relive my happy, exciting times as I explored my passions.

An unanticipated result of completing this memoir is that I have made a decision to be less of an introvert. I have chosen to share many stories in this book for the first time. In the process of writing, I asked myself the question, "Why now?" When I reflected on my rich family history, I realized that nothing was documented. My only source of information was my Aunt Marjorie (my oldest living relative at seventy-nine) who has begun to suffer from memory loss. I realized that I wanted to leave a record for my children and generations to follow.

The second reason why I so passionately shared these never before heard stories of my life is to encourage the young adults to whom I minister. As a pastor, when others share their personal pain and journey with me, they often do not think that I understand. Like the time a teenage girl shared with me the story of her rape. Weeping, she said, "Pastor, you would never understand." I shared brief details of my own teenage rape ordeal with her. My story helped her to face and speak out about her own story. What she did not know was that I had not, until then, shared this story with anyone. Even then, it was done in one sentence: "I know what you are going through because it happened to me." It helped her to know that her pastor understood because she, too, had a similar experience.

Recounting my rape experience, as you would imagine, was the hardest topic for me to write in this book, but in so doing, I felt I would help others and continue to heal myself. When young people read this book, I hope that they, too, might not be ashamed to share their own experiences and get help without making the same mistake I did of waiting a lifetime. When parents read my book, and, in particular my rape experience, it is my hope that they will be more open in discussing these issues with their girls and boys.

I wrote this book because I wanted end-time church planters to know that they do not have to have a perfect tract record for the Lord to use them as an instrument of change. I have heard many women, despite their willingness to step out in ministry, decline because they have been divorced or have had a child out of wedlock. Some of them were made to believe by their religious leaders that they are not good enough. I have been through all of that, including failed relationships. If the

Lord could use me, read my story, and allow the Lord to use you.

I found the collections of advice from clergy in Chapter 9 useful as I navigated ministry in South Florida. I spent long hours doing these interviews and compiling my data in the hope that this record could be useful to those non-traditional church planters, who like me, defied the odds to follow the call of the Lord on their lives.

Winning souls for Jesus is still my second order of business, my first being to continue to develop my personal walk with Christ. Like the apostle Paul, I do not want to find myself in the bind of preaching to others while I, myself, become a castaway. I often think about the three young boys who entered the tent crusade with, no doubt, bad intentions, but left with Christ in their hearts after they accepted Jesus. Since then, I have truly come to terms with learning to love and share the gospel anywhere and anyplace without shame or fear. I could have remained hidden behind the drum set and missed my golden opportunity to allow the Lord to use me in touching the hearts of those three teenagers that day.

Some days in my imperfection and weakness as a human, I resented doing street ministry because of the rejection that often comes with it and the pain of processing that rejection. However, I could not give up because the pain of the effort was immeasurable compared to the rewards.

My life story is far from finished, but as I stay the course, I have learned two important lessons, take responsibility for my actions and be humble. My avid prayer and fasting routine kept me in tune with the Lord and reality. I am still faced with the challenge of maintaining a disciplined prayer life and balancing life's demands, but my desire to worship and spread the Good News of Jesus Christ is the driving force that keeps me going.

If I were to sum up my overall direction in life, I would agree with the words of King Solomon as he reflected on his life in Ecclesiastes 12:13: "Let us hear the conclusion of the matter: Fear God, and keep his commandments: for this is the whole duty of man" (KJV).

Bibliography

Einstein, Albert. *The Expanded Quotable Einstein.* ed. Alice Calaprice. Princeton: Princeton University Press, 2000.

Hinn, Benny. Sermon in May 2001.

King, Martin Luther Jr. *A Testament of Hope: The Essential Writings and Speeches of Martin Luther King, Jr.,* ed. James Melvin Washington. New York: HarperCollins, 1991.

Nee, Watchman. *Ministering to the House or to God?* Anaheim: Living Stream Ministry, 1993

Yonggi Cho, David. *Successful Home Cell Groups.* Alachua: Bridge-Logos Publishers, 1999

Request or Comments should be addressed to

Pastor Dianne Van der Meer
Post Office Box 272757
Boca Raton, Florida 33427
or
Email: Vandermeerdee@yahoo.com
outonalimb1@comcast.net

Phone: 877-876-2415

About the Author:

Author Dianne Van der Meer was born on the island of Trinidad in the West Indies and has also lived in England and the Unites States of America. She discovered her writing skills as she sat on her porch, overlooking the ocean, in Quincy, Massachusetts.

Dianne worked in Massachusetts in various departments of state government. She served as a research analyst in the Massachusetts House of Representatives and with the Massachusetts Board of Regents of Higher Education. Dianne Van der Meer taught in an adjunct capacity at both private and public institutions of higher education in Massachusetts. She answered a call to ministry and, after years of serving as a lay minister, was ordained as a pastor.

Pastor Van der Meer is the founder of Living Water Christian Fellowship Church and has birthed a campus-based ministry in Boca Raton, Florida. She was a visiting chaplain at Boca Community Hospital and was recently married. Pastor Van der Meer is a voting member of the

Investigative Review Board at the West Boca Medical Center, a hospital in Boca Raton.

Endnotes

1 *American Heritage Dictionary,* 4th ed., s.v. "Modern dance."

2 *Merriam-Webster Collegiate Dictionary,* 11th ed., s.v. "Spoil."

3 *Wikipedia, the Free Encyclopedia,* s.v. "Thatcher, Margaret." http://www. En.wikiquote.org/wiki/Margaret_Thatcher (accessed April 29, 2008)

4 *Webster Dictionary,* 1st ed., s.v. "Crossroad."